"Mama, it ain't over 'til the pink marble comes."

A true story of triumph over life and death.

Sandee Williams
with Jeanne Todd

Hannibal Books
P.O. Box 461592
Garland, TX 75046

www.hannibalbooks.com

This is the revised, second edition of
"*Mama, it ain't over 'til the pink marble comes*"
first published in 1994 by Hannibal Books.

Printed by United Graphics, Inc., Mattoon, IL
Cover design by Mark Counts
ISBN 0-929292-74-X
Library of Congress Control Number: 2004109926

Dedicated to the memory
of my best friend.

With love,
Sandee

To one of God's best musical servants!
From: Gene Williams
Rom. 12:1,2
2006

To order more copies of *"Mama, it ain't over 'til the pink marble comes"*

Contact:
Hannibal Books
P.O. Box 461592
Garland, Texas 75046-1592

Fax: 1-972-487-7960
Phone: 1-800-747-0738 or 972-487-5710
Email: hannibalbooks@earthlink.net
Visit: www.hannibalbooks.com

Order form in back of this book.

Table of Contents

Chapter One

Mama in the Mausoleum

TRAFFIC AROUND ATLANTA WAS LIGHT on this Sunday afternoon in the spring of 1992. Mama's usual zest for life showed in her smile as we chatted about everything but the business at hand. Seeing the Covington exit, I steered my 1991 white Blazer in that direction. Ahead, just off the Interstate, stood the Lawnwood Memorial Park. Warm sunshine showed off white and pink dogwoods and cherry trees holding onto their last blossoms.

A kind, soft spoken man introduced himself as David Jernigan. "I'm Mrs. Gene Williams and this is my daughter, Sandee. We're here for me," Mama told him bluntly. "I have terminal cancer."

It was obvious he hadn't had many clients like Dorothy Williams, for it took a few seconds for him to regain his composure. "I, uh, I'm very sorry about, er, your illness, madam."

"You don't have to fret for me," Mama interjected. "I'm prepared."

"Yes, yes, of course."

"Would you take us around the cemetery?" Mama asked.

"Of course, of course. Why don't you follow me in your car?"

Although he showed us various plots, nothing was quite what Mama had in mind. Just then, we noticed a stately mausoleum overlooking the grounds from the crest of a gentle hill. "Mama, why don't we take a look inside there?" I suggested.

"All right."

With David leading the way, I wheeled the Blazer up the rise and stopped under the covered terrace of the southern colonial manor. David opened my door then walked around to assist Mama.

Mama merely let him hold the door. She slid out of her seat and began walking smartly toward the tomb. Ever the southern gentleman, David moved ahead to hold the front door for us. "As you will see, he noted, the mausoleum is not quite finished."

Mama and I walked into the vault room. Our eyes swept over the light teal walls. "Well, what's it going to look like?" Mama asked, without any show of discomfort. "I've got a great imagination."

"There's going to be a large chandelier above us, and we have some mauve carpet coming in. We're going to place a couple of chairs down here for visitors. And, oh yes, we've ordered this pink Italian marble to seal each vault, but it's not here yet."

"Hmmmm," Mama said. I could almost see her imagination sliding into high gear. She quickly spun around and faced me. "Sounds like my kind of place, Sandee."

A smile darted across our guide's face as Mama continued her query. "Now tell me, David, how much do these vaults cost?

"Our prices vary with the different levels, madam. There is the `Kneeling Level,' the `Touching Level,' and the `Head Level'." Motioning toward the very top, he said, "But the least expensive is the `Heaven Level'."

"Well." A frown creased Mama's forehead as she looked heavenward. "Just how would you get me way up there?"

"Oh, that's no problem. We have a crane to hoist you. . . .."

Mama's laughter interrupted. "With my luck, the crane would break, and I would bounce all the way down the hill, casket and all." I couldn't help laughing, too.

This dear man looked at Mama as if she had lost her mind. I don't think he had ever before had a terminal client selecting grave sites with such gusto.

After studying the room a bit more, Mama pointed to the vaults near her shoulder height, and asked, "What level is this?"

"This is the `Heart Level'."

"Yep," Mama nodded to me, her decision made. "That

sounds like the level I need to be on."

After we signed the purchase agreement, Mama and I headed home. "Remember, Mama, we've agreed that you can't quit fighting this cancer until I say its okay."

"Y-e-a-h." I could tell she wondered what I was thinking.

"So . . . you can't die `til that pink marble gets in from Italy. Besides, there'd be no place to put you."

"Well, that's right." She nodded. Her laughter filled the car.

"Yeah, Mama, it ain't over `til the pink marble comes."

But I'm getting ahead of myself. Mama was a great story teller and she would have wanted me to start closer to the beginning.

Chapter Two

Mama as the Pastor's Wife

FOR AS LONG AS I CAN REMEMBER the warmth of Mama's freckled, smiling face and her tender arms of love transformed wherever we lived into a home. Mama's flowing, dark auburn hair completed her beauty like a crown. Ben Rogers, Dad's long-time friend, called her a cross between Lottie Moon, a saintly Baptist missionary, and the actress, Lucille Ball.

Our family made up the background. First, Mama and Dad. Next, me, their firstborn and only daughter. Later Randy, four years my junior. Then, Tim arrived during my twelfth year and smiled his way into our hearts.

Grandparents, too, had their place in our world. Mama's parents, Mammaw and Pawpaw Fiew—pronounced like view—were warm, generous and loving. Dad's parents divorced in the early 1930s, and this brought great chaos to our family for many years. After his mother, Iola, married Sam Miller, she prevented her seven-year-old son from seeing his father. Sam became known to the grandchildren as Sampaw; Dad's mother was known as Mammaw Miller. During his student days at Baylor University, Dad sought and found his own father, Henry Williams, who was then married to Alma.

But most of all, Mama fills my early memories.

I remember that every Saturday evening, Mama got all our clothes ready for Sunday morning church. She placed my ruffled dress, hairbows, lace-top anklets and shiny white patent shoes on a chair beside my bed. Once Mama was sure Dad's white shirt and suit were ready, she pressed her dress. As she worked, Mama smiled at Dad. He had been a preacher since before I was born and often rocked me as he read aloud from a theology book. I listened just as if he were reading *The Three Bears*.

Mama loved being a minister's wife. But until Dad graduated from Baylor University and then moved us from New Orleans Seminary housing to the rough little river town of Pearl River, Louisiana, Mama didn't know that being a minister's wife might mean calling on the FBI.

Dad, a six-foot Texan with thick black hair, was still a student at New Orleans Seminary when Pearl River's little Baptist church called him as pastor. He'd been pastor of a small church in Elm Mott, Texas while in Baylor. This was a larger pastorate.

Young and enthusiastic, he and Mama set out to share the gospel with everyone they met. Soon, the whole town knew them by name. They fondly called Dad "the funeral preacher," because he held such short services.

After we had been there a while, people from all over this southern lumber town, some from the wrong side of the track and several families of "river rats" who resided along the Pearl River, started showing up at the church for services. That didn't set well with the old, we've-never-done-it-that-way-before members with better incomes. They didn't like the changes these newcomers made in their church.

About this time, Mama and I went to visit her parents, Mammaw and Pawpaw Fiew, in Alvin, Texas. Dad stayed behind to tend his flock.

"Why doesn't Gene call?" Mama kept asking. "I'm sure he's all right, but I'd feel better if I could talk to him."

Just then Pawpaw's truck pulled into the driveway. He came stomping into the house and grabbed me up in his sweaty arms. "Give yer ole Pawpaw some sugar, little Sandee."

I smacked him on his rough cheek and he turned to Mama sitting by the phone. "Well, Dorothy, you talk to ol' Gene today?"

Mama shook her head. "I keep hoping he'll call. I'm about ready to call him."

"Go ahead," Pawpaw said. "Be our guest."

Mama dialed and held the phone to her ear. I ran over to talk to Dad, too. To Mama's surprise, a lady answered our ring. She attended the Pearl River church and shared our party line. Mama exchanged a few words with her and hung up. Mama didn't speak about what they'd said, but I could tell something was not right.

Mama got Dad on the phone the next morning. She explained about the lady answering the phone the evening before. "Gene, I think you're being watched. You'd better be real careful."

When we arrived back in Louisiana, I could tell Mama was glad to get home. She looked in the mail box and found an unsigned letter addressed to her in very proper English. Years later Mama told me what it said:

"Your husband has acted improperly. Check his behavior last Thursday evening. We are not going to put up with such behavior by our preacher. If he knows what's good for him, he'll leave Pearl River. If he doesn't, we'll expose him to the whole church."

Mama burst out crying. I was too young to understand why, but I could tell something was wrong when she showed the letter to Dad. He shook his head and began hugging her. "It isn't true! It's a malicious lie, Dottie!"

"I know it is, Gene." Sobs broke into Mama's words. "But what, what are we going to do?"

Suddenly I was afraid. Tears streamed down my cheeks as I grabbed Mama around her legs. Mama lifted me to her lap as they looked at the letter some more.

"Let me see that date again, Dottie." Then Dad grinned. "Well, whoever wrote this knew I wasn't home on that night, but they didn't know where I was."

"What do you mean?" Mama's shaky voice asked.

"Well, the night I was supposed to be `misbehaving' is the night I had dinner with Doc and Mrs. Burnham. After I left their house, I went to see a couple of church members who got caught electrocuting fish in the river." Dad smiled broadly. "I signed in and out of the jail. All of my time on that night is easily accounted for."

"Gene, I think I know this handwriting." Mama sounded like

herself again as she wiped her eyes and nose, then reinspected the letter. "I'm going over to the church and get some reports. I'm guessing the writing on them will match this."

"Good. I need to run and get some gas in the car. Sandee, would you like to come with me?"

I stood in my usual spot behind his right shoulder as we rode. Suddenly I realized Dad was sobbing. "Daddy, why are you crying?"

"Well, honey, some people are trying to make your daddy look bad." Pulling his handkerchief out, Dad wiped at the tears puddling down his cheeks.

"Well, let's just go beat `em up." To my two-year-old mind, that would take care of those mean people.

Choking back his laughter, Dad said, "Honey, you just can't go beat up people because they hurt you." Then Dad rolled down his window and we started singing *This Little Light of Mine* as we headed to the Texaco station.

Mama's guess about the handwriting proved to be right. "I'll take this and show the deacons," Dad said grimly once we were back home.

When Dad went to the Saturday night deacons' meeting, the men were outraged at the letter's contents. That is, until they went home and discovered that the wife of one of the deacons wrote it. Dad knew he had nothing to hide, so he tacked the letter on the bulletin board in the church foyer the next morning. Sunday services proceeded as usual, but some people avoided speaking to our family. Soon, the town was buzzing.

One townsperson after another voiced support later that day. "Accusing you like that was a terrible thing for someone to do," they said.

"Who wrote that letter?" two visitors asked at once, without waiting for an answer.

"You ain't the first preacher from that church that they tried to run off," one old grizzled face told Dad.

That night, Mama and Dad talked, trying to come up with a better way to prove what they suspected. "If we just knew a handwriting expert," Mama said. "Someone who could compare the documents and prove the same person wrote both."

"That's what we need all right, Dottie."

All at once Mama brightened. "How about the FBI?"

"Well," Dad hesitated, "I don't know if they do that sort of thing."

"You know, they have an office in New Orleans, Gene. Would it hurt to go down and see if they could help us?"

"I suppose we could see."

"I'll call Mrs. Burnham. I know she'll keep Sandee for us tomorrow, while we run into New Orleans. She, Doc and some of the other church people want our names cleared as much as we do."

"Well, Dottie, if the Burnhams can keep Sandee, we'll go. In the meantime, let's pray for guidance."

Young as I was, I knew Mama and Dad trusted each other and God enough to get through any trouble spot.

The next morning, Mama and Dad headed for the FBI office. When they returned, they told the Burnhams and other supporters how two agents listened to the whole story. After seeing the ledger and the letter, the agents looked at each other and shook their heads.

"We're very sorry, Reverend and Mrs. Williams," the first man said. "You see, unless your lives were threatened, the FBI can't help you."

"I understand," Dad said. He and Mama stood up to leave. "Well, thank you for taking time to hear us out."

"You know," the second agent spoke up. "Maybe just saying you'd been here to see us would frighten this person off."

Dad brightened. "Yes, it might be worth a try."

On the way home, Mama and Dad chose two people they could share the news with about consulting a handwriting expert at the FBI. As expected, within a couple of hours, the news swept through the whole town.

One day the next week, Dad rushed into the house for lunch, smiling. "Dottie, you won't believe what just happened."

"Tell me." Mama scooted my chair up to the table, then turned her eyes on Dad.

"A long, black car pulled into Pearl River and parked along the main drag. Three men in dark suits stepped out. Mrs. Burnham said they never cracked a smile as their eyes looked this way and that. Next thing she knew, those men were flashing badges to the people standing around."

"What happened next?" Mama's eyes danced as much as Dad's.

"One of the dark-suited fellows asked, `Can you tell me about an unsigned letter to the Baptist preacher?' "

"Oh, no," Mama frowned. "Who were they, Gene?"

"Well," Dad chuckled, "I'm not sure, but I think and the whole town is convinced that they were the FBI."

"What happened next? Are the men still here?"

"No. After a few minutes, all three of them got back into their long black car. They drove past the church, waved at me, then pulled out of town. Believe me, they sure put Pearl River's grapevine to humming."

"Well . . .." Mama was so busy laughing that she didn't finish her sentence.

We never did find out why the agents came to Pearl River that day. Mama and Dad always figured the FBI was just passing through town and decided to help out the young preacher and his wife the only way they could. One thing was sure. Their visit ended all threatening letters to Dad.

Then and ever after, Mama never did suspect Dad of doing anything improper with another woman. It was the same with Dad about Mama. They giggled over the Pearl River episode many times. But I always knew that, behind the giggle, Mama recognized God's hand in sending the FBI to protect Dad's reputation.

Dad was still a seminary student when he and Mama decided to leave Pearl River. His next church was in Loxley, Alabama, about 165 miles east of New Orleans. Since our family would go there just on weekends, Mama happily settled us into one of the seminary's new brick apartment buildings. Mama was good at making adjustments when the Lord called Dad to a new church. Besides, the apartment was more modern than the Pearl River parsonage.

The next Friday afternoon, Mama watched Dad load our luggage before the three of us piled into our 1951 Dodge. We had just enough gas to get us to Ocean Springs, Mississippi. There, Dad turned off the highway and pulled into a service station.

"Fill'er up?" the smiling attendant asked.

"Yes, sir." After the gas tank was filled, Dad got out to talk to the man who washed our windshield and checked the oil. I noticed that he had a mustache yellowed from tobacco juice.

"Where you headed?" the attendant asked. Dad explained that he was a seminary student on the way to his church in Loxley.

Mama and I talked inside the car. My fingers traced around the little butterfly-shaped metal box on my lap. My birthday silver dollars just did fit under its purple satin-covered lid. I always knew the ten silver dollars were mine and that anytime Mama "borrowed" them, she would give them back. Our budget was tight, and Mama had already explained that she needed my ten silver dollars to buy gas for this trip.

"Sir?" Dad approached the attendant when it was time to pay for the gas. "I'd like to ask a favor of you."

"What is it?"

"Well, if I pay you with ten silver dollars, could you give me change like it was a ten dollar bill?"

"That's no problem."

"When we come back through Sunday night, I'll have my pay from the church. Would you be able to hold those silver dollars and let me redeem them then? You see, they're my little girl's."

"Well," the man looked inside the car and smiled at me, "I don't see why I couldn't do that." I'm not sure I fully understood what was going on when I opened my butterfly box so Mama could remove the dollars, but I knew I was helping. The man counted the silver. Then looking back at me, he told Mama, "I'll take good care of these for your little girl."

Mama spent Saturday getting us settled in our weekend home

and meeting new people. Mama's smile seemed to put each visitor immediately at ease.

After Sunday morning service we had dinner with one of the church families. On Monday we got back into our Dodge and headed for New Orleans. "Are we there yet?" I asked, after what seemed like a long time. "Are we almost to the man who has my silver dollars?"

Finally, Dad pulled into the gas station in Ocean Springs. The man with the yellow mustache was working. When he saw us drive in, he waved.

"How was your weekend?" he asked, filling our gas tank.

"Just great." Dad paid with a twenty-dollar bill given to him by the church treasurer. "Thank you for helping us out."

"Glad to do it." The attendant returned my ten silver dollars and some change to Dad. "Any weekend you need to use that silver for travelin' money, I'll keep it fer yuh."

Dad passed the silver through the open window to Mama, and she handed it to me to put back in my little butterfly box.

"Thank you, Sandee." Mama's smile made me feel warm and good inside. Then, happily riding between Mama and Dad, I played with my full butterfly box until my eyes could no longer stay open.

Dad preached in Loxley for about two years. That Ocean Springs gas station became our stopping place on many Friday and Sunday evenings. True to his word, the mustached attendant kept my silver dollars safe during the six-or-so times we needed to use them. And Mama, true to her word, saw that they were returned to me every time.

Mama always kept her word to me. That was something I never doubted.

Every Saturday found Mama and Dad visiting in the Loxley community, sharing Jesus with all the country folks who would listen. Just as in Pearl River, people came to know the Lord and were baptized.

Often Dad learned of a nearby local church which had shut down. Always generous with his time and energy, Dad would load Mama and me into our Dodge the following Sunday afternoon, as he searched out a member of this church. Hot dust blew through open windows and onto our faces as we bounced over dirt and gravel roads between houses. When Dad knocked on a door, then disappeared inside the house, we knew he'd found the right person. During their talk, Dad promised to send a student preacher to this congregation, if they would just keep the church open.

Mama's white handkerchief was soon sweat stained from wiping our faces as we sat in the car, waiting for Dad. We sang choruses, read books and colored to pass the time. Sometimes Mama breathed, "It's so hot in this car. Why does he do this?" But, knowing Dad felt this was what God wanted him to do, Mama never asked him to stop helping student pastors connect with local churches.

Back at the seminary, Dad continued his ministerial matching. When our poor Dodge started complaining about all the miles we'd put on it, Dad looked for something newer. Soon we were making our trips in a Ford—but still without air conditioning.

In the meantime, the Loxley church kept growing. You see, Mama and Dad accepted it as truth when their Bibles said, "Whosoever will may come." They hadn't yet understood that some people don't want really rich folks or poor folks in their churches. Again, like at Pearl River, the old, ruling hands started getting nervous at the sight of change. Mama and Dad didn't notice. They just kept witnessing.

When our vacation time came the next summer, Mama, Dad and I went to Texas to visit kinfolks. What a surprise we got on our return.

The old hands at the Loxley church thought they had found a way to win their church back while we were gone. They called for a vote on the preacher to decide whether or not to keep Dad as pastor. However, when word got out, all the people Mama and Dad had led to the Lord made sure they were present to cast their votes.

The vote came down in Dad's favor. To Mama, that outcome showed God's pleasure with their work. So she and Dad kept loving the Loxley people. Dad continued preaching what the Bible said, and the church kept growing. After that, Mama often smiled and said, "No preacher's worth his salt unless he's been voted on at least once."

God blessed Dad's leadership and Mama's help in the churches he pastored while in school. The little church in Elm Mott, Texas, then the one in Pearl River, Louisiana and the Loxley, Alabama church. Each grew to the point of never requiring another student pastor after Dad left them.

Mama had been so pleased when Dad received his Master's degree in 1953. Now, in May of 1955, she was even prouder as Dad became the first and only student at the New Orleans Baptist Theological Seminary to earn his doctor of theology degree in twenty months.

Green Oaks Baptist Church in Baton Rouge, Louisiana, issued a call for Dad to come be their pastor. He and Mama talked it over and prayed together before deciding to accept. Then they talked to me about the move.

Even though I was only four-years-old, I'd already lived in several houses. I knew it didn't matter where we lived as long as Mama and Dad were there, it was home.

As for Mama, it was "whither thou goest, I will go. . .. With Mama, where we lived wasn't nearly as important as knowing she was with Dad and in the will of God, doing God's work.

Chapter Three

Mama as Dad's Helpmate

MAMA'S JOY OVERFLOWED as we settled into the brand new, two-bathroom, built-for-us pastorium at Green Oaks. Dad was busy and happy with a growing church. Playmates were close by for me.

Mama began to ready a nursery for the baby expected in August. As we folded newly laundered diapers and tiny undershirts, Mama said, "Sandee, look at these cute little clothes. Won't it be fun to help take care of your new baby sister or brother?" Then, with a hug, she added, "But, Sandee, Mama will always love you."

With school days behind and a full time pastorate, it was time to trade-in our high-mileage Ford for another car. Mama, probably thinking back to those hot Alabama Sunday afternoons, laughed as she told Dad, "Gene, I don't care if the car has four wheels or not, as long as it is air conditioned."

When Dad brought home a two-tone green, four-door, air conditioned Chrysler, Mama clapped her hands with joy.

Life seemed just about perfect.

Then one August night, Mama's hug and kiss interrupted my sleep. "Sandee, Daddy's going to take you over to spend the night with Mrs. Smith next door."

"Why, Mama?" I grabbed my Rock-A-Bye-Baby doll and tried to rub the sleep from my eyes as I nestled against Dad's shoulder. I liked Mrs. Smith, but this seemed like a funny time to visit her.

"I'm going to go get our new baby," Mama said, kissing me once more. "Daddy will come after you in the morning, darlin'."

Mrs. Smith met us at the door with a smile, then Dad disappeared into the dark. Something just didn't feel right about this.

Taking my hand, Mrs. Smith asked, "Would you like some grape drink and some popcorn, Sandee?"

In my mind I thought, *No, I want my Mama*. Instead I said, "Sure," as a plan to escape began to unfold in my little mind.

As Mrs. Smith got distracted with making the popcorn in the kitchen, I sneaked over to the front door and turned the knob to unlock it. Even though I was afraid of the dark, I raced across the yards and into my garage. There, through the screen door, I saw Mama lying on the couch rubbing her huge stomach. Suddenly I remembered overhearing Mama talking to her mother on the phone. "I'm so worried about this baby. It hasn't moved in months. The doctor tells me that it is just fine, but I think there is something wrong." A pained expression filled Mama's face. In that instant, I knew she was dying.

I opened the door and ran into the room just as the phone rang. Dad bolted from his chair at the sight of me, then went to answer the phone. I heard him say, "Yes, she's here. I'll bring her back over."

Dad picked me up once more and crossed the yards again. "Sandee, you need to stay at Mrs. Smith's while we go get your new baby brother or sister. Everything's going to be all right."

This time I stayed put, but I didn't believe everything was "all right" even when Mrs. Smith tucked me in the huge soft bed. I remember pulling the covers over my head, but sleep did not ease my worried imagination.

The next morning, I sat on the porch listening and watching for Dad. Finally, he pulled our car into the drive. Arms outstretched, I hurried over. "Daddy. Daddy."

"Hi, honey," Dad lifted me for a hug and his whiskers scratched my face. His eyes were red and he looked terrible. All at once, I was afraid that my worst fear had come true: Mama had died.

"How's Mama?" I managed.

"She's fine," Dad said, patting my back. As I watched his face, a slow smile stretched across it. "And, Sandee, you have a new baby brother."

A brother? Whew!

"Yes, Sandee. Mammaw Fiew is coming to take care of you while Mama is gone for a few days. Then, you and I will go to the hospital to bring Mama and the new baby home. Won't that be fine?"

I still wasn't happy that Mama was gone, but at least I knew she was all right and what was going on.

Mammaw Fiew arrived later that day for a two-week visit. She played "Candy Land" and "Uncle Wiggley" with me, and I helped her do laundry and clean. As we worked and played, Mammaw told me how sweet and cute my brother, Randy, was. She explained how I could help Mama with him. Soon we were ready for them to come home.

Dad and I waited while a nurse helped Mama and Randy out to the car. An orderly carried Mama's suitcase and flowers. "Hi, darlin'." Mama hugged me tight when I grabbed her knees. "Just a minute and you can see your brother."

Dad ushered me into the back seat while Mama settled herself in the front. I watched as Mama placed the squirming blue bundle on a pillow between her and Dad. Then she pulled one corner of the blanket back.

"Randy, this is your big sister, Sandee." Mama smiled at me. "And, Sandee, this is Randy."

Randy looked like a wrinkled little bulldog, with jowls hanging down. When the sun hit his face, he started kicking and screaming, and he fussed all the way home. I remember looking over the front seat, thinking, *Do you mean we went through all this trouble to get this ugly baby?*

Mama and Dad gave me lots of hugs and a box of presents over the next few days. I hurried to bring bibs, diapers and blankets when Mama needed them. Sometimes I got to sit in the big chair and hold Randy. Soon, I decided he was all right, after all.

For Randy's first Sunday at church, Mama dressed him in a blue turtleneck outfit. He still looked like the-prize-fighter-who-lost. I felt very important, helping with the diaper bag.

One friend after another rushed up to Mama, eager for a look at the new baby. "Oh, isn't he cu . . . Oh, he's sweet!"

"We know he isn't pretty," Mama repeated to each one. "But we're going to keep him anyway."

Of course, everyone laughed.

And, by the time he was three months old, Randy was as cute as Mama knew he would be.

Mama's contentment bubbled over as she cared for Dad, Randy and me. It was still a thrill for her to go into downtown Baton Rouge, select a new dress and hand her first-ever charge card to the department store clerk. "Oh," often the clerk would say, to Mama's joy. "You're Dr. Williams' wife. I've heard him preach. He's good."

All around us, houses were springing up and new people moving into the developing Green Oaks area. Our church kept growing, too, as Dad marked his second anniversary.

Before long, Dad and others from our church came up with an idea for reaching more of our new neighbors. Arrangements were made to hold a tent meeting a few streets over from Green Oaks, with Dad as the evangelist. Mama rejoiced with Dad when, at meeting's end, there were enough new people to start another church. To help them, ninety members from Green Oaks joined our neighbors to establish what became Stevendale Baptist Church.

Seeing people respond to Dad's preaching made the struggle of seminary seem worthwhile to Mama. Every day, her smile grew brighter as she settled more into her role as a suburban pastor's wife. She liked it.

So, Mama was not prepared for the earthquake Dad delivered a few weeks later. "Dottie, I think the Lord is leading me to resign as pastor of Green Oaks. I believe God is calling me to full-time evangelism."

"Oh, Gene!" Shock waves shattered Mama's happiness. Big tears streamed down her cheeks as she sank to a chair.

Mama's first-class pity party had begun.

She made sure Randy and I were all right as we played with the neighbor kids. Then, even in her misery, she started moving furniture, sweeping and dusting. Years later, she laughed and told me how every self-pitying thought made her work all the harder. And how it was hard to tell where her thinking left off and her praying began. *"Just when we're getting a little ahead, Lord, Gene wants to go back to living on an uncertain, shoe string income. Only now we have a two-year-old and Sandee's almost ready to start school. What will become of us?"*

Finally, as Mama knelt to scrub the bathtub, her tears outnumbered the drops of water running into it. *"Here, Lord, we struggled to get Gene this doctor's degree, and if there's anything an evangelist doesn't need, it's a doctor's degree. Why did we do that?"*

Suddenly, Mama got up off her knees, eyes open and hands outstretched. *Now, God, You have got to speak to me about this. Show me, if this is of You. You know Gene doesn't even look the part, he isn't one of those evangelist types.* That's when Mama said she tried picturing Daddy dressed in the common evangelist's garb of the day: white suit, purple shirt and white shoes. Suddenly a laugh escaped Mama. *Lord, do you realize? He doesn't even own a white suit!*

With her laughter, the pity party ended. She knew, if Dad was to be an evangelist, she would be right by his side.

Usually, by this time of year, Dad had a number of revival meetings booked. To date, he had none. Using human logic, going into full time evangelism did not make sense at this time. Finally, he and Mama decided to seek wisdom from others before making a final decision.

One advisor said, "You should save up $5,000 for reserve."

"You ought to have a year of meetings booked, before setting out," others urged.

"If you go into the little churches," another evangelist said, "you will always be a little church evangelist, because the big churches won't have you."

Good, practical advice. Yet, as Mama and Dad prayed for guidance, they discovered this was not God's formula for them.

Their finances would not allow the cash reserve suggested. Dad still had no bookings. And, Dad told Mama, "My Bible says to do with all your might whatever God gives you to do.

Whether its in a big or a little church."

So, Dad surrendered to God's call, Mama followed and the Lord gave them peace in their decision. As for the hard-earned doctorate turning some churches off, well, they just had to trust God, knowing He had said, "Get the degree."

Mama often said, "My trust was not only in God, but also that my husband was listening to God as he should."

By the time Mama told me we were moving out of the parsonage, she was ready to point out the positives. "Just look, Sandee, you get to have bunk beds in your new bedroom. Since you're the oldest, you'll sleep on the top, and Randy on the bottom. Won't that be great?" And, to me, it was. It didn't matter where we lived, as long as Mama and Dad were there, too.

Once again, we packed up our belongings.

Years later, I realized how hard it must have been for Mama to move from our lovely new home into a little rented shotgun house in Baton Rouge, with only one bathroom and no garage. Yet, once she decided it was the right thing to do, she made this little house our home.

Mama and Dad became members of Immanuel Baptist Church and enrolled us in Sunday school. Our neighbors, Harvey and Vivian Smith and Jim and Jewel Osborne, were members, too. While we played with their children, Mama and Dad got to know these two couples better. Friendship deepened as they visited in each other's homes. Soon they were sharing struggles and joys with each other.

Not long after that, Immanuel was scheduled for revival services with J. Harold Smith as the evangelist. Dad looked forward to talking with this veteran preacher. "Dottie," he hinted strongly to Mama, "I'd sure like to invite J. Harold to lunch one day during our meeting."

"So would I, Gene, but we're almost broke. I don't know how we can buy enough food to feed him and us, too."

"Well, if we're supposed to have J. Harold here, the Lord will show us how to do it."

Later, while discussing the situation with their friends, an idea sparked. "Oh, wouldn't that be great," Vivian said, looking at Jewel. "We don't have the china or crystal, and we don't have the dining room table . . .."

"But, Dottie, you and Gene do," Jewel finished. "So, if you will use your table and set up your china, we'll bring the food."

Mama breathed, "Thank you, Lord."

The men agreed and plans quickly fell together for spending a lunch hour with this respected man of God.

Finally the big day arrived. Laughter and joy filled our home as good friends shared what they had with each other and their guest. Mama's eyes still sparkled after the others were gone. "Oh, Gene, isn't God good to us?"

J. Harold Smith had offered words of encouragement to Dad. Still, he and Mama had no idea what their future held. But, together, they sought God's guidance and waited for more invitations from pastors for meetings.

"You know, Gene, your mother's house would be big enough for us until you get established in evangelism," Mama said, as they talked again of where God wanted them.

"And, Houston should be a good location for me. I still know a lot of people there."

Mammaw Miller and Sampaw had recently moved across Houston to a new home off Homestead Avenue. They still owned the typical 1930s, buff brick bungalow at 1522 Dunlavy Street, near the River Oaks area. A two-car garage stood toward the back of the tree-shaded lot. Mostly older people lived in the quiet neighborhood, but an elementary school was only four blocks away. Although the house was not air conditioned, the tall trees which lined the street helped provide a cool breeze.

Mama listened as Dad phoned his mother about renting her house to our family. Mama sat by looking anxious for she knew how unpredictable Mammaw Iola could be. But Dad hung up the phone with a broad smile. "Dottie, how would you like to live in Houston?"

"Well, Gene, wherever you go, I go."

That sounded great to me. We'd been there on vacation, so I already knew my way around the neighborhood. But the best part of all was that Randy and I would have our own bedrooms again. "Thank you, Lord," I whispered.

Mama, practiced at moving by now, began organizing and packing. Before long our furniture was in a couple of U-Haul trailers headed toward Houston. An air of excitement hung about this move.

No sooner were we settled than our phone began to ring for Dad. Preacher friends from New Orleans Seminary had learned he was in evangelism. "Our church is not very big, Gene, but we'd like you to come preach our revival," one after another said. Soon Dad's calendar was dotted with meetings. God began to use Dad even though he didn't have a white coat or look the part of an evangelist.

Mama and Dad joined First Baptist Church of Houston. Knowing Dad would be out preaching most weeks, Mama valued the new friends she found there. Randy and I made friends, too.

Revival meetings usually lasted a whole week, and sometimes Dad was gone for four weeks in a row. The business end of Dad's ministry and household duties fell to Mama since she was Dad's secretary, office manager and chief-cook-and-bottle-washer.

Mama saw the home operations as a vital part of the ministry. If she could keep the office and the household running smoothly, Dad could better keep his mind on winning people to Christ. Then when Dad was home, he could spend more time with Mama, me and Randy.

Dad depended on his revival offerings to support our family. Many of his bookings came from pastors he had put in touch with needy churches when they were in seminary. Later, Mama would often remark, "During those early years in evangelism, we couldn't have paid the bills, without those young pastors and their little churches. And, Gene, I thought you were out there wasting gas on those hot Alabama Sunday afternoons!"

We never missed a meal. To Mama, our limited food budget was another opportunity to exercise faith. She was a good cook and served Randy and me nutritious, but often meatless, meals. Like most kids, we considered meals an interruption to our play, so it didn't much matter what we ate. When Dad was home, Mama always served meat and made sure the meals were satisfying. I'm sure he thought we ate like that all the time.

I didn't realize until much later why Mama adjusted our meals that way. She told me, "One thing I never wanted to do was make Gene feel he was not providing well for us."

Once their decision was made to go into evangelism, it was important to Mama that nothing sidetrack Dad. Mama saw this as a way to undergird Dad's ministry and keep the home fires burning.

Mama was Dad's true helpmate.

Chapter Four

Mama and the School Bureaucracy

MAMA, DECIDING TO GIVE MY SELF-IMAGE A BOOST, worked all summer to create pretty school dresses for when I started third grade. Loose threads and cotton scraps lay scattered under our dining room table, near the Singer's foot pedal, after each session. Even tomboys like me wore dresses to school everyday, back then.

Mama proudly hung five new puffed-sleeve dresses in my closet. Each was a different color and had a full, gathered skirt with a sash that Mama tied into a pert bow at my back. My, they were pretty.

On the day school began, I danced with excitement as Mama helped me into the red dress. My blonde ponytail bounced against my neck as I kissed Mama's cheek. Then I hurried off to Woodrow Wilson Elementary School, eager to see old friends. From there, things started downhill.

During recess we played tag. The boy who was "It" grabbed my sleeve and accidentally tore it from my shoulder. "My dress," I sobbed as the playground assistant tried to console me. "Mama worked so hard to make it for me."

"Oh, honey," Mama said, hugging me tight that afternoon. "What happened to your dress?" She listened closely as I choked out my sad story between sobs. After wiping my eyes, Mama inspected my torn sleeve. "Well, don't worry, Sandee," she assured me. "Mama can fix it. Just be more careful next time."

Mama should have saved her breath. On Tuesday, my foot caught in the black-and-white plaid's hem and pulled the skirt loose at the front waist. A jagged limb poked a hole in the back of my green dress as I climbed out of a tree on Wednesday. Thursday, I was really careful and made it all day without messing up my dress. Pleased with myself, I decided to take the shortcut home. I wanted Mama to see I had made it with my dress intact.

The path I followed cut through some yards before coming out at the street just a block from our house. *Wow*! I thought. *One more block and I'll be home. Surely I can make that without anything else happening*.

Just ahead, a big black car was parked at the curb. I don't know how it happened, but suddenly the car bumper reached out and grabbed my dress. R-i-i-i-p.

When I looked down, a big hole gaped in my skirt, just below the right patch pocket. I choked back a sob and started running toward home.

"I'm so glad you're home," Mama said, smiling and opening the door. Her eyes took in my quivering chin, then swept across my Thursday dress as I ran into her soft, freckled arms. She hugged me close and my sobs broke through. "Honey, I know you don't mean to ruin your clothes. Tell me, what happened to your dress today?" For the fourth straight day, I told my story of destruction, and Mama comforted.

Finally, it was Friday morning. Even as Mama smoothed the white collar of my last new dress, I decided, *forget it!. Four days is enough. I'm not going to be careful anymore*. "Come on," I called to the imaginary horse I mounted. "Let's go."

Behind me, as I started riding the four blocks to school, I heard Mama sigh. "Maybe the horse will protect her dress today." Mama's wish came true. Thanks to the imaginary horse, the fifth dress arrived home without a single rip.

What Mama and I didn't realize then was how those four torn-and-patched dresses were a token of things to come that year. No matter how hard I tried, I could not please solemn Mrs. Grouch, my grouchy teacher.

About two weeks after school started, my reading group moved our chairs into a circle with Mrs. Grouch. Reading made me nervous. Listening closely and studying the pictures, I followed as the first two recited. Then, as always, my imagination and I read the assigned paragraph.

As the next girl continued, Mrs. Grouch's eyes seemed to hold on me. My palm felt damp as I brushed a stray hair from my forehead. Then it was my turn to read again.

Mrs. Grouch shook her head as she listened. My insides quivered. I knew she had discovered my secret.

"Sandra." Her eyes seemed to bore holes in mine. "You cannot read. You'll have to move to the lowest reading group."

My stomach turned flip-flops. Suddenly my worst nightmare had come true. Not only did Mrs. Grouch know I couldn't read, but everyone in my class knew, too.

A week or so later, Mrs. Grouch, worked her way around the classroom, helping with long division and multiplication. Her thick body stopped at the boy ahead of me. Then, without a pause at my desk, she bent her purple-gray bouffant hairdo toward the girl behind me. Since I had a question, too, I turned around in my seat. "Mrs. Grouch, can you help me?"

"No, honey." Her words cut deep inside me. "There's no use to help you. You're retarded."

Retarded! The awful word slammed into my brain. My face flared as the other third graders snickered. *If only I were invisible right now*, I wished.

Instead of being a fun time, I now dreaded recess. "Hey, Stupid," my classmates called out. And, "Don't play with her, she's retarded." Not once did anyone silence them. The more I heard that I was stupid or ugly, the more insecure and fearful I felt. When school was out I struck out for home. Immediately.

Mama wiped my tears each afternoon, as we talked. She kept telling me I was pretty and smart. Over and over, she showed how much she loved me. But, by now, my sleep had decreased to two-or-three hours a night. My giggle was gone and, head down, I trudged to school each day.

Looking back, I know that I was showing classic symptoms of depression. But, in the late 1950s, no one was admitting children could be depressed.

Several times, as Mama waited outside the building for me, Mrs. Grouch's shrill, impatient voice had traveled through open classroom windows to Mama's ears. Once, when Mama walked in the classroom to talk with Mrs. Grouch, my teacher quickly closed her desk drawer. But Mama had already caught sight of the bottles of "medicine" inside.

The one thing that kept me going was knowing Mama believed in me and was trying to figure out how to handle this problem. And I knew she was praying for me.

"Good morning, Sandee." Mama's voice was soft as she gently coaxed me awake one Friday. Opening my eyes, I saw her familiar smile. It pushed little wrinkles into her fair-skinned cheeks. "Today, instead of school, we're going to get all dressed up and celebrate your `national holiday'."

Now, Mama's national holiday had nothing to do with the nation, and all to do with her child's need for love and comfort.

Our big day began with Mama handing Randy over to a baby sitter, then taking me to lunch at Felix's Mexican Restaurant. Young as I was, I knew my parents didn't have money to take a kid to lunch there. We talked and laughed about all sorts of things. After we ate, Mama even splurged on a Mexican lollipop for me.

Then, at the movie theater, Mama bought the cheapest seats for newly-released *Ben Hur.* The whole place was empty except for us, but we sat in our assigned, top-row-of-the-balcony seats. Every once in a while, Mama and I would look at each other and smile or she would pat my hand. Just being around Mama gave me a warm, secure feeling inside. Whatever was going on at school, I knew Mama was still pleased that I was her girl.

The next week, my head was bent over a math assignment when Mrs. Grouch commanded, "Sandra, stop that humming."

I jumped, then sat looking at her. *Was I really humming?* I wondered. I didn't dare ask, so I went back to work.

"Sandra," I heard again, "stop that humming, now!" But, since I didn't realize I was humming, I couldn't stop. All this music just poured out of me, like steam through an escape valve. Finally, my teacher sent me to sit in the hall for the third time.

Soon after this, it was time to take our first six-week report card home. Mama looked at my grades and conduct report, then hugged me tight. "Something's wrong here. We've got to find out what. I know you're not stupid."

More convinced than ever that Mrs. Grouch was a big part of my problem, Mama phoned the principal. A couple of days later, the principal stood near my teacher's desk, watching us work. An uneasy feeling crept over me as they stepped back to the front to talk quietly.

"Sandra?" Mrs. Grouch ordered. "Please come up here."

The principal asked me lots of questions about school. My breath caught at her final question. "Sandra, do you like Mrs. Grouch?"

"Yes," I lied, "I like her." How could I tell the truth in front of her?

A meeting was called for Mama, Mrs. Grouch and the principal. Mama didn't tell me right away what they had said, but I knew she didn't like whatever it was. I'm sure Mama's eyes sparked when she heard their verdict. "We're sorry, Mrs. Williams, but Sandra is retarded and will never make it out of the eighth grade."

"Well," Mama shot back, "if my daughter is retarded, she became that way at this school. She was not retarded before coming here."

"Gene," Mama said to Dad by phone later that day, "I'm going to insist that Sandra be tested for reading ability. I think it may be the answer to her problems at school. Besides her teacher, that is."

When the principal refused to have me tested, Mama looked for another way. Dad's aunt, a teacher at another elementary school, knew a woman who was familiar with this new field. She agreed to give me a battery of reading tests privately.

Her patience and kindness made the two-hour session go easily. Mama sighed with relief when the results proved her right. My IQ was high. But somehow the letters and words got mixed up between the page and my brain. The bottom line was, I could not read. Instead I looked at the pictures and made up my own story.

With a better understanding of my problem, Mama began searching for solutions. One of the things she discovered was that I had a lazy eye (amblyopia). The result of this great news was that I had to wear thick glasses and a patch over my right eye. Not only did half the class think I was retarded, now I looked the part.

Mama and Dad were also seeking God's guidance in this. After all, they had never before walked this path as parents. Not long afterward, Dad met a reading teacher in a Houston area church where he was holding a revival. He sought her counsel. After hearing my case history, this fine Christian woman shared with Dad that she was more than a reading teacher. She was the principal of the Houston Independent School District Reading Clinic. Even though my grades were too good to qualify me for her program, she fought the bureaucracy, saying, "I don't care what her grades are, the child can't read." Thank goodness, she helped rescue Mrs. Grouch's "retarded student."

Mama spent hours with me after school, helping me do eye exercises. She helped me understand I was smart not dumb or retarded. My reading improved, and she kept me at grade level.

Mrs. Grouch and the principal at my school refused to accept the outside diagnosis. They were upset that Mama had gone around them to get the tests done and prove them wrong.

Then, as other parents also voiced their displeasure with Mrs. Grouch, something good happened. All the children whose parents had complained were pulled out of her room and placed in Miss Rose's third-grade class. Best of all, our new teacher was gentle and kind. I sensed right away that she was interested in healing my hurt. She even let me hum in class. She and Mama helped me believe that I could learn.

Yep, I wouldn't have survived school except that Mama fought for me and won.

Chapter Five

Mama and Nesting

MAMA WAS AN ONLY CHILD who grew up in the oil fields of south Texas. I loved watching her face grow soft and her eyes sparkle as she told me about it. Somehow, it helped me know she and Dad loved me as much as Mammaw and Pawpaw Fiew had loved her.

Whenever Mama said, "I had about the best growing up anybody could ever have had," I knew her story was beginning. Even after I knew it by heart, I loved to sit back and listen.

"My daddy worked at one well until the oil played out. Then he loaded all our belongings, Mother and me into our old Ford coupe. I always got to sit between them, as we talked and laughed our way across dusty roads to the next work site. Once Daddy was hired, we'd find a little apartment or trailer-house to rent in the town closest by.

"On Sundays, our family always went to the First Baptist Church of whatever town we were in. Mother had been a Christian since she was a child. Then at age seven, during a revival meeting in Edna, Texas, I accepted the Lord as Savior. Soon after that, my daddy did, too.

"The first school morning we were in town, Mother walked me to the brick schoolhouse and signed me up for my grade. She always volunteered to be room mother, or help however she could. I think that's part of why I never minded moving. My mother made it seem like the most natural thing to do. And, she showed me how to make friends by being friendly to others.

"I always had the prettiest cotton dresses to wear, because my mother was a good seamstress. Sometimes, she and I looked in catalogs and stores or display windows for ideas. I sketched my favorite ones, and she made them on her portable Singer."

Mama always smiled at the memory of how she looked. "Oh, but, Sandee, my pretty cotton dresses almost caused a problem one time."

"When, Mama?"

"My second year of high school, we moved way down to Ramondville, Texas. That tough little town's population was about half Mexican and half Gringo. On my first day in school there, I discovered I was the only girl wearing a dress. The other girls had on T-shirts and blue jeans, just like the boys." Mama's familiar giggle filled my room. "I didn't know what to make of that. I had slacks, but I didn't own one pair of blue jeans. Up to then, the only people I knew who wore blue jeans were people on horseback."

"What happened, Mama? Did they like you anyhow?"

"Oh my. They gave me a hard time." Mama frowned and shook her head. "Some of the girls wrote ugly things about me on the bathroom walls. When I walked by, they stopped talking or snickered and I knew they were talking about me."

"What did you do?"

"Well, I looked around. Pretty soon I noticed some girls who weren't part of the `in' group either. I started talking to them, and before long, we were having fun in our own group.

"Now, the other girls knew that the boys thought I was awfully cute in my dresses. So, by the time Daddy's job was done and we left Ramondville, almost every girl in that school was wearing a dress, too."

Mama laughed, then continued. "I almost never went a whole grade at one school. In fact, by high school graduation I had gone to seventeen different schools. Yet, one year I was a cheerleader. Another year I was the `little ol' red headed girl playing that big bass drum' in the band at football games.

"You know what?" Mama looked me in the eye as our laughter faded. "Playing that bass drum taught me something. It doesn't hurt to do something ridiculous every once in a while."

When I was in my teens, I asked Mama, "Were you ever a rebellious teenager?"

"W-e-l-l, uh, I went through a time when I wanted to do what I wanted to do and eat what I wanted to eat. I remember one Saturday morning when I announced to my mother that I didn't want what she had prepared for breakfast. Instead, I fixed my own breakfast, and it was wonderful. I had fresh yeast rolls and my favorite cucumbers and vinegar. It was so good that I ate a double portion. It wasn't until an hour later that I realized my serious mistake."

"Why, Mama, what happened?" Already, I could see a twinkle in her eye.

"Well, my stomach began to swell. It got bigger and bigger and bigger. You should have seen me I must have looked like I was about seven months pregnant. I believe, if someone had stuck a pin in my stomach, I would have blown right up. Mother and I both absolutely panicked. She gave me a carbonated powder concoction to drink, knowing that if it didn't give relief I would have to go to the hospital. Finally, I went out and ran around the house hoping for an atomic bomb. Luckily, the fuse blew. And, I learned something. Doing what you want to do is not always the thing to do. Mother's breakfast would have been much better for me."

Mama saved this part of the story until I got a little older. "Years ago, most little Texas towns had a brothel in them. On numerous occasions, my mother would catch one of the `ladies' out in the yard and talk to her. Mother had such a sweet countenance that she won a number of these prostitutes to the Lord. When that happened, Mother took the `lady' to church the next Sunday and she sat with us. Sometimes the regular church members got upset and walked by us without even speaking. That's part of why I was called `oil field trash' as a child. I guess, by definition, that's what we were. After all, Daddy did work in the oil fields and we moved from town to town, according to where the work was. But it didn't bother me a bit when they called me names. Mother and Daddy had always made me feel that I was wonderful, even when I was a three-year-old child and bald as an eagle. From birth, I had never grown any hair. Yet my parents made me feel I was the best thing since sliced bread. My mother and daddy had done such a job of helping me to know who I was, that ugly words just rolled off me like water off a duck's back. Later, when I remembered what that person had said, I'd think, *Well, you just don't know me*."

Always, Mama told how Mammaw Fiew passed on the importance of making a nest for her family. Every time she told me her story, it ended with, "As long as Mother, Daddy and I were together, all was right with the world. Where the nest was didn't matter. Home was the people who lived there."

Looking back, I thank God that He special-picked Mama to learn in childhood all the lessons she'd need for when she became an evangelist's wife and a mama. Not only did Mama learn those lessons, but from those experiences she passed on wonderful parenting skills to those around her.

Since Mama had grown up in a family where love and concern flowed freely, openness was the norm for her. Problems were to be discussed, solved and dispensed with.

Dad, too, came from a fine family. His maternal grandparents were involved in his life just as Mama's were in hers. But, somehow, Dad's mother, Mammaw Miller, came out of that family different from all the rest. Mammaw's parents, brothers and sisters were all loving, caring, emotionally healthy people. Yet Mammaw Miller was a manipulator who sought to control and rule everything and everyone around her. She often used rage to manage people. When that didn't work, she had a fainting spell. Mama picked up real fast that Mammaw Miller's purpose was to get Mammaw Miller's way. Mama said that once she saw this, she understood where Dad got his hot flashes of temper. Mama also understood Dad's great fear of being controlled by his mother or anyone else. This fear of vulnerability affected his willingness for emotional intimacy. Thus Mama had her job cut out for her. She would love her husband in the way she wanted to be loved, thereby teaching him how to love. She proved to Dad that love was safe. It was selfless, not selfish.

Now the extent of Mama's experience with fit-throwers before Iola Miller came into her life was slim-to-none, and slim left town. I remember Mama giggling and telling me, "When I was young, my family used to laugh about a cousin's fit throwing. To cure her, they took the cousin outside and threw her in the horse trough!"

I think Mama might have considered that with her mother-in-law, but there was no horse trough where Mammaw Miller lived. Besides, I don't think it would have made any difference.

Mama's first experience with Mammaw Miller came just before her wedding. Mammaw called Mama's dad and instructed him to tell his daughter she was forbidden to marry Gene Williams.

Pawpaw Fiew calmly listened to her and said, "If you can keep your son from marrying my daughter, I can certainly keep my daughter from marrying your son."

Mammaw was furious. She knew that even though she had picked out a fine River Oaks girl for Dad, she could not keep him from marrying this oil field trash.

As wedding plans progressed, Mammaw Miller continued to create chaos. Mammaw did not like it when, despite all her earlier efforts, now-adult Dad continued to pursue a relationship with his father. She had even tried to alter Dad's identity, when he was seven-years-old, by changing his surname from Williams to Miller. Now, just before his marriage to Mama, Dad decided to take back his father's name. In court, his name was changed from Gene Miller to Gene Miller Williams. So it was not surprising that Mammaw Miller tried to forbid Dad's father from attending the wedding. But when she started to complain about the color of Mammaw Fiew's dress, Mama had had enough.

Early on the wedding day, Mama took a long walk to reevaluate whether or not she wanted to marry into Dad's family. It was not an issue of whether she loved Dad, but was this really what God wanted for her. The longer she walked, the more impressed she became that God was truly in this, and that Dad had the strength to protect her from all harm, including his mother.

As Mama started back toward her parents' home, she saw her own mother dressed and standing in the front doorway, looking frantic. "Where have you been? You're about to be late for your own wedding."

Mama merely smiled and said she'd been having a little discourse with the Lord.

Except for the photographer forgetting to put film in the camera, the rest of the day went off without a hitch.

Knowing only God could give the help she needed, Mama sent heavenward many prayers for Dad and their marriage. She asked the Lord to please help Dad overcome the dysfunctional life his mother had created. Then one day, near the end of their first year, Mama had cause to wonder which way their marriage was going.

Dad looked around the living room for a book he'd been studying. It was not in or under his chair, or the table beside it. He knew Mama was in the next room, and called, "Dorothy, what have you done with my book?"

"What book is that, Gene?"

"You know the one I mean." Dad's voice grew louder, more intense. "The one I was using to study. Where is it? What have you done with it? How can I study if you keep moving my books all the time?"

Mama sensed anger growing in Dad's voice as she walked across the living room toward his chair. Dad had never before spoken to her like this. Mama thought, *His tone sounds just like his mother's. If I didn't know better, I'd say Iola was here*. By now, Mama stood in the middle of the living room.

"Gene, what is my name?" She later told me that she wasn't old enough or smart enough to know what to do, so God must have given her the wisdom she had requested. "Look at me, Gene. What is my name?"

"Your name is Dorothy," Dad snarled.

"I don't think you believe my name is Dorothy." *Stay calm,* she told herself. Then she insisted, "Look at me, Gene. What is my name? Who am I?"

"Dorothy!" Dad exploded. "You are Dorothy!"

"Gene, I'm sorry that your mother hurt you and yelled at you as she did, but I haven't done those things. <u>I am Dorothy</u>."

Dad stared into Mama's face for a few seconds. Then without a word, he got up and left. Mama held her tongue as the door slammed shut behind him. She remembered thinking, *A man needs time to think things through*. Even this early in marriage, she had learned that Dad's answer after thinking would be different from any answer she would immediately demand.

With no idea how long Dad would be gone, Mama busied her hands with cleaning. Prayers filled her thoughts as she worked. Two hours passed.

Finally, she heard the door open. "Dorothy," Dad said, taking Mama in his arms. "To the best of my ability, I will never do that again. If I forget, you remind me. God helping me, I will never treat you as my mother treated me. Because her way is not right."

Right then, Dad started "cutting his garbage from the past," as Mama put it. What could have broken their relationship, instead created a bond of strong mutual trust that became the cornerstone of their marriage.

From that day forward, Dad entrusted Mama with teaching him how to love. And Mama renewed her trust that Dad would listen to God and follow in the right direction.

Together, Mama and Dad decided to honor his mother, as God's Word taught, without letting her destroy the joy in their lives.

The first real confrontation between my mother and my grandmother came shortly after my birth.

Mama told me how, at my life's beginning, I was about to be a breech birth. Instead of a C-Section, the doctor decided to turn me. Mama said she then continued into her second day of labor. All the nurses except one were kind and gentle. But one battle-axe nurse hurt her with each exam. Mama was sure she had been an army nurse in WWII. Nonetheless, during one of this nurse's exams Mama told her, "None of the other nurses hurt me when they examine me. If you hurt me one more time, I'm going to kick you across the room." To Mama's delight, all further exams were pain free.

Because of the difficult delivery, it was several days before

Mama and I got to go home. Mammaw Miller was there on our arrival. It didn't take long for her to have a temper tantrum. When my twenty-year-old mama heard Dad leave the house, she painfully struggled to get to the living room. There, she confronted her mother-in-law for the first time.

"Iola, this is my home. If you ever throw another temper tantrum, have a fainting spell or act ugly in my home again I will throw you out the back door, and your luggage behind you. Then I will take your granddaughter to a place where you'll never find us. And I will give your son the choice as to whether or not he comes with us. I think you know what he will choose to do."

Nothing more was said. For the first time, Iola had met her match and she knew she couldn't win against Mama. From that point on, in Mama's home, Mammaw Miller never acted inappropriately again.

That was good, because after our move to Houston, we saw Mammaw Miller often. Mammaw knew her Bible and taught a Sunday school class. But her mood changed from one minute to the next, and she had definite opinions about everything. Obviously believing her views were correct, she defended them vigorously. Sampaw, Mama's step-father-in-law, was a kind man who stayed out of his wife's way and took her in stride.

For as far back as I can remember, Mammaw gave me small gifts for no reason. She made a big deal out of my birthday and always gave me extravagant Christmas gifts. Yet she all but ignored Randy's birthdays and gave him small Christmas presents.

"Look what I have for you, Sandee," Mammaw called every time I saw her. In her hand was candy, a jump rope, a ball and jacks or a pretty pair of socks.

"Oh, thank you!" I loved surprises, and wrapped my arms around Mammaw's neck.

When I was almost nine and still having school problems, Mammaw began taking my side against anyone with whom I disagreed. I also began to notice that her gifts came with an emotional price tag. In return, Mammaw wanted me with her all the time. At times she said things to show me that she could care for me better than Mama could. At first I felt bewildered, then I got angry at her. What I didn't know then was how closely Mama and Dad were separately watching. Mama later told me of talking to Dad about what she saw happening.

"Gene, you may think I've lost my mind but I think your mother is trying to steal Sandee away from me."

"I know. I hoped you hadn't noticed," Dad said, to her surprise. "I've been watching it very closely. Dorothy, Sandee is your daughter. There's an awful lot of you in her, and I think she will take care of this by herself. But if she does not, I will intercede."

Dad's wisdom and Mama's trust in him proved true. Once I recognized Mammaw's presents as the bribes they were, I refused to continue her game. Mama allowed me to experience manipulation and learn that I had a choice in its outcome.

"Sandee," Mammaw still invited, "come spend the night at my house."

"I can't tonight," I said, thinking what excuse to make. "I promised Randy we'd play checkers."

Her mouth drooped to make a sad face. "Well, Sandee, if you really love Mammaw, you'll come spend the night." After a while, when the guilt trips didn't work, she eased up on the pressure.

Whenever Mammaw Miller acted up, Mama respectfully discussed it with us. She helped us understand that Mammaw was a sick person. And that her kind of love said, "I love you, so do things my way." Always, Mama encouraged us to respect Mammaw, while showing us that there was a better way to handle things.

Mama was good at setting clear boundaries for acceptable behavior, yet she never forced Randy and me into the same mold. For instance, I talked like a parrot while Randy, a thinker, didn't open his mouth unless he had something worth saying.

Mama allowed us freedom to learn from and even fail in situations at home. To do that, she constantly put us in the position of decision making. Like the day Mama took Randy and me across town to visit Mammaw Miller's sister, Aunt Fran.

"Well, Randy," Aunt Fran said, as Randy played with his food at dinner, "aren't you hungry?"

"I don't like your food," my matter-of-fact brother said.

Good natured Great Aunt Fran smiled at his impertinence. "Oh, I'm sorry, Randy." She offered to bring something else to the table for my little brother, but Mama asked her not to.

We visited a while that afternoon, then headed home. "Son," Mama corrected Randy, as she drove. "You were rude to Aunt Fran. You were wrong to tell her you didn't like her food, and I don't want you to behave that way again."

Randy's face reddened and tensed in anger. As soon as Mama pulled the car into our driveway, Randy charged toward the house. I watched as he somehow misjudged the door's opening, and rammed his head into the frame. Dazed, he fell backward as Mama and I got out of the car.

I didn't know whether to laugh or cry.

Mama's eyes had followed Randy's every move. She must have figured he was not seriously hurt because, without missing a beat, Mama stepped over him and walked on into the house. As I reached the door, Randy jumped up and ran after Mama.

"Mama, I was hurt." Randy looked puzzled as he rubbed his bump. "Why did you just walk over me?"

Mama focused her full attention on him. "Randy, you must not get so angry that you don't know what you're doing. That will only cause you to hurt yourself or someone else."

"Yes, Mama, I was mad." I could almost hear his thoughts processing what had happened. "I was very mad."

Mama must have chosen the right moment for teaching Randy. His temper never flared like that again.

Privacy became important to me. I was big for my age and developed early physically. Besides that, I was tired of my little brother roaming in and out of my territory all the time.

"Randy," I warned my brother. "Don't come into my room unless you knock first."

Mama heard me repeat my demand several times, but she never said a word to me about it. She knew I liked to use the short cut through Randy's room into the rest of the house.

A few days later, I was headed from my room to the bathroom when four-year-old Randy blocked my path at his door.

"You make me knock, so you have to knock." His dark eyes sparkled. "If I can't come in your room, you can't come in mine."

I screamed and yelled, but Randy wouldn't budge. Hearing the noise, Mama stepped to where she could see us. Her smile told me that she had patiently waited for my passive, brown headed, little brother to out-think me. And he had.

Mama didn't need to say a word. She knew I had learned my lesson.

Chapter Six

Mama and Family Togetherness

IT TOOK THREE YEAR'S of Mama's careful budgeting before Dad was established as an evangelist and we made it through a Houston winter without borrowing money. While family finances had eased a little, we were about to outgrow our little home on Dunlavy.

Mama and Dad began talking about buying a new house. We all knew it was just a dream. Mama and Dad didn't have enough saved for a down payment. Nonetheless, we began to dream about what this house would be. Dad wanted four bedrooms, Mama wanted air
conditioning, I wanted a dishwasher and Randy wanted a park to play in. We all wanted a fenced-in yard with lots of trees. Surely this was just a fantasy, but Mama always said it was fun to dream.

Mama, as had long been her habit, prayed about things as they came to mind during her daily activities. She called this walking with the Lord. A new home was added to her list. Dad's prayer and devotion time was more formal, but his travel schedule was so erratic that it was hard to have regular family devotions. Still, we all agreed to seek God's will in this matter. And they began looking at houses on the market.

Dad's week-between-meetings was our family time. It was a tribute to her nestmaking that Mama capitalized on the time available for the family by cherishing every single minute. Any needed work on house or car she completed while he was gone. Mama laundered Dad's clothes without a complaint. She packed his suitcase for each trip, making sure everything stayed as neat as possible. Mama was the one who booted Dad out the door, saying, "God called you to evangelism. We'll be right here when you get home."

Looking for our dream house took every available free minute. There was no time left for us all to be together, so Dad called a family meeting, as was our habit. As we knelt together, we reminded the Lord of our shortage of space and the features we desired in a new house.

"Lord," Mama prayed, "You've never failed us yet. So we are giving You this house and this dream. We're letting it go. We trust You will show us the home we are to have, even if it's our little house on Dunlavy. We thank You for providing what is best for us."

As we all said, amen, Mama smiled and Dad smiled back. Randy and I went back to our bicycles.

Mama worried about Dad's shoes. They were very old and had holes in the bottoms. While on the platform, the holes could be seen when he lifted and crossed his legs. To Mama's delight, a man gave Dad a new pair of shoes. Mama proudly packed them in the suitcase for Dad's next meeting. On his return, the shoes were not there. Dad had given them to someone who needed them more.

"Okay," Mama teased, "but, don't cross your legs any more while you're on the platform."

That September, a lady interested in supporting Dad's work in evangelism gave our family a calf. Mama's meals with three-pounds-for-a-dollar ground beef were great, but the thought of roasts and steaks set our mouths to watering. Mama loved to tell what happened after that.

Before we even had time to butcher that calf, Dad went to a "Mt. Zion" camp meeting. He listened as missionaries from many areas shared stories and showed slides of the work they were doing. Some, who were outside a Southern Baptist sponsored area, needed to travel and raise funds while back in the United States. Otherwise they couldn't continue reaching people with the gospel on their mission field. The only car available for their use was old and worn out.

Dad knew God wanted him to help these missionaries. But

how? They needed money and Dad had no cash to spare. *Lord,* Dad prayed, *I'm willing. Just show me what you want me to do.*

And God did. God must have prepared Mama for Dad's return, too. "Dottie," Dad glowed, "I know we needed that beef, but God impressed me to help those missionaries. I gave them our calf."

"That's good."

"I also gave them our air conditioned Chrysler, and promised them my next love offering."

"Now, that's all right, Gene." Mama drew in a big breath and swallowed. Then her eyes sparkled, "But the day you come into this house and tell me that you ran into an old preacher who needed a wife and two kids, I'm going to draw the line."

As we all laughed, I remembered numerous times I'd seen a very lonely Mama stop in the middle of sweeping floors or cooking to pray for Dad. "And Lord," her prayer ending echoed in my mind, "please give me the grace to follow my husband and peace in my heart while doing it."

I knew I'd just seen Mama activate that principle.

Dad's next love offering arrived September 10, 1961. It barely touched Dad's hands before it was on its way to the missionaries.

With the Chrysler gone, our little green, un-airconditioned Opal moved up to only car status. It was our $700, Preferred Risk wonder that didn't smell of smoke from its previous owner. "Here comes Mrs. Williams' little popcorn popper," the mechanics teased whenever Mama took it for servicing. But the popper got us around.

A short time later, Dad was scheduled for a meeting at Clay Road Baptist Church in Houston's Spring Branch area. A group of church ladies invited Dad and the pastor to a luncheon after Monday morning services.

After lunch, one of the women began to excuse herself by saying, "I'm sorry, but I have to leave. I have an appointment to show some property."

Dad's ears perked up. "You're a real estate agent?"

"Yeah, I sell commercial."

"I see." Dad paused. "Well, I need a house."

"What kind of house are you looking for?"

Dad told her about our dream house. In detail. They shook hands and the lady left for her appointment. Dad continued talking with the others.

Tuesday morning, when Dad started down the church aisle to his place at the front for the noon service, he heard, "Good morning, Dr. Williams." He turned to see the smiling face of the real estate woman. She offered her hand and pressed a business card against his palm. Then she took her seat and Dad walked on to his.

When Dad flipped her card over, he saw written across its back, "I have found your house." Dad's heart beat a little faster as he wondered what God had in store. Then he put the business card into his pocket and brushed those thoughts aside. He was there to deliver God's message.

The real estate lady approached Dad as he finished greeting people after the service. "Would you like to see your house? It's on Peppermill not far from here."

"Oh, yes." Dad and the pastor headed with her to her car. As they drove off, he asked, "If you're in commercial real estate, how did you find this house so soon?"

"God found the house. As you dreamed, the house has four bedrooms, a living room, dining room, huge den, and kitchen with a breakfast area. It's air conditioned and the builder installed top grade carpet and light fixtures." The real estate lady pulled her car to the curb. "Well, Dr. Williams, here we are."

Dad's eyes feasted on the sight. Oak trees and Japanese Yews set off the brick one-story house and its attached two-car garage. Thirty or more trees shaded the back patio area, and a redwood fence enclosed the manicured back yard.

"It is a lovely place," Dad said. "But it looks like more house than we can afford."

"Let's go inside and look around, then we'll talk about that," she said, with a quiet smile.

The house was not elegant but was well built and roomy. "It was custom built," the realtor explained, "by a lady who had just lost her husband. She only lived here a year."

Just then, looking from the living room window, a soft whistle escaped Dad. *How did I miss that*? Across the street was an entire city block covered with trees. "There's Randy's park!" Dad exclaimed.

"What do you think, Dr. Williams?"

"Dottie needs to come see it. This house is exactly what we asked God for and more." Dad said, with amazement. He walked out to the back yard and knelt among the trees.

Lord, I could not imagine having a house like this. Show me, Lord, what You would have me do. Give me wisdom. If this is the house You have for us, then I claim it right now in the name of Jesus.

A few days later Dad called another family meeting. I could tell by Mama's expression that something was up. Dad indicated that we had something we needed to pray about, and Mama began to describe the house she had inspected. "It has four bedrooms, lots of trees, air conditioning and a redwood fence." Mentally, we began to check things off our list.

Randy jumped in and said, "Does it have a park?"

"Right across the street," Mama exulted. "And the garage is so huge that we could drive our little green Opal in and turn it around with the garage door closed."

"What about a dishwasher," I asked.

Mama looked at me with a mischievous twinkle in her eye. "Well, honey, we already have a dishwasher. I thought you were our dishwasher."

"But I'm a gas dishwasher. We need an electric one."

"Well, the house has an electric one, too."

We knew that this was not our house yet, but we prayed as a family that God's will would be done. We also knew that we were okay no matter where we lived. Even if we lived in a cardboard box.

Mama and Dad never got an opportunity to place a bid on the property. Instead, the widow made us a proposal: She reduced the house $4000. Mama and Dad would have a year to pay $500 down. Then the seller would hold the loan at six-percent interest. Lastly, we would only have to pay monthly interest of $100 and $10 on the principal.

We accepted her offer as manna from heaven. But then Dad said to Mama, "What if we can't make the payments?"

"Well, if we can't make the payment, we'll just sell those Japanese Yews."

With money so tight in Dad's line of work, the question still remained: where would the $500 come from. He and Mama agreed in prayer to allow God to work out the details.

"If this is the house God wants us to have," Mama and Dad reminded each other, "He will work this out, too."

God's timing is always unique. A week before the $500 payment was due, a friend came up to Dad at one of his revivals. "I don't know why God has told me this," Billy Watkins said, "but he has instructed me to give you this check."

As Dad looked at the check, he realized it was for $500. He smiled at Billy. "I know exactly why God told you to do this."

But God wasn't finished yet.

A man who knew Dad had given away our Chrysler called. "I'd like to buy you a brand new car. But only if you'll promise that you will not give it away."

"If you give it to me," Dad assured him, "and you specify that I can't give it away, I won't."

"Go down and pick out whatever you want," the man instructed Dad. "Get one with everything on it. I'm not going to be happy if it isn't loaded."

Mama and Dad settled on a brand new Buick with all the accessories. And, the man paid cash for it.

Now we had a brand new house and a brand new car that God had given us. After that, I knew just what Mama meant when she said, "You can't out-give God!"

In June of 1962 we headed west for the annual Southern Baptist Convention. For several years, we had spent part of each summer camping and traveling with Dad, while he preached at meetings. This time, Mama, an expert camper by now, drove Randy and me from Houston to San Francisco in our car. These were days when a woman felt safe traveling cross-country with only her children. Behind us followed our tent-camper. Its customized closets kept our clothes, especially Dad's suits and shirts, neat and ready to wear.

Dad had been invited to preach a week-long meeting at First Baptist Church of San Francisco and was already in the Golden Gate city. We were to meet him at his hotel.

Our whole trip had been one beautiful nature scene after another. Now, seeing the majestic redwoods almost took our breath away. Once we found our campsite, Mama parked and unhooked the tent-trailer. Randy and I helped, but we could hardly wait to tell Dad all about our adventure. Mama seemed pretty excited, too.

We would stay in the hotel with him until his meeting closed on Sunday. Then the annual convention of our big denomination began. Since our family couldn't afford the hotel rates, we planned to stay at the Samuel P. Taylor State Park, north of San Francisco during the convention.

Sunday morning, we went to hear Dad preach in that beautiful old church. His sermon about hell had us almost feeling scorched. It was not a typical Sunday morning sermon.

As we waited for Dad near the hotel lobby elevator that afternoon, a lot of preachers we didn't know stood around. From their talk, we could tell they hoped last-minute cancellations would open up rooms for their stay at the convention hotel.

"Were you at First Baptist this morning?" one asked the others. Mama and I looked at each other, wondering what these men would say about Dad.

"Yes, I was," one man replied, as the others nodded. "The church was full of convention people, wasn't it?"

A third one said, "Did you ever in your life hear such a message? Preaching about hell, on a Sunday morning?"

"I wonder why he preached <u>that</u> message to us?" the first ventured.

"Well, you know," another spoke up, as though he could explain it all. "He's from Texas."

Mama's hand flew over her mouth as she whispered, "Maybe they needed to be reminded of hell, too," before she started laughing. "Besides, when your daddy preaches on hell, it's because God told him to. Not because he was from Texas."

As Dad helped us set up our campsite on Monday, another camper pulled in near us. To our amazement, we recognized the pastor of Houston's posh River Oaks Baptist Church, Dr. Denman and his wife. They got busy, helping their two teenage sons set up camp. Then, after a short time inside the camper, Dr. Denman stepped out, dressed in a nice suit and tie. A gorgeous, large hat preceded Mrs. Denman's exit from the tent. Her outfit was complete with lovely jewelry and a fur. Off they went to the convention in their car, leaving their sons to enjoy camping while they stayed in one of the hotels.

Later, as we walked around the convention hall, Mama and Dad renewed friendships with seminary friends and other preachers. Many of them had had Dad for meetings in their churches.

For some reason, one of the favorite ice-breakers in convention conversation is, "Where are you staying?" When a preacher put the question to Mama and Dad, Mama replied in pretended solemnity, "At the Samuel P. Taylor, near Dr. and Mrs. Denman." Somewhere in the sentence, in a lowered tone, Mama added, "State Park." Of course, many didn't hear that part, but the park was named for Mr. Taylor.

"I see," the preacher replied. "Glad you're doing so well."

It was important to appear prosperous, because no one wanted an unsuccessful evangelist. However, Mama and Dad's prosperous look was the result of careful planning and shopping. Mama could always look like a million after spending only ten dollars on clothes at Houston's Bargain Gusher. Dad had long purchased nice cars second hand, after someone else paid for the first half. Then, because they considered themselves stewards of God's money, Mama and Dad took good care of what had been provided.

After the convention, Dad took us to Yosemite National Park. Randy and I explored and saw everything we could. Then we traveled and camped for several more weeks where Dad had meetings scheduled.

One night as I drifted off to sleep on a camp cot, I overheard

Mama and Dad talking about the future. "You know, Dottie, now that the kids are a little bigger, I hope you can travel more often with me."

"Oh, yes, Gene. It will be great for us to have more time together."

I remember smiling as sleep overtook me, secure in the love our family shared.

Chapter Seven

Mama's Surprise

UNTIL NOW, MAMA HAD A GOOD CRY about once a year and that was it. But, for the past week, she was tearful every time I looked at her. I knew she missed Dad, but his being away preaching had not been a problem for her before this. Obviously something else was wrong.

Mama came to me a few days later. "Sandee, I'm sure you've wondered about all my tears lately. Let me tell you about the big surprise Daddy and I just got. We're going to have a new baby."

"Oh, Mama!" Excitement burst inside me. Then I remembered all of Mama's tearful days. *Should I be happy or sad?*

"It's not that I don't want this baby." Mama smiled through moist eyes. "It's just that a new baby will change some of our plans. You know how little time Dad and I get to spend together. Well, with a new baby, I'll have to start over with diapers and bottles. I won't be able to travel with him like we had hoped. That's why I've been on a pity party."

With that, Mama started talking about the joys a new brother or sister would bring to our family.

Later that day I overheard Mama talking to Randy. "Wouldn't it be nice for you to have a baby brother or sister? Why don't we pray for a baby brother or sister?" Since I knew a new baby was already on the way, this seemed a little strange. But Randy accepted her challenge.

"Guess what, Randy," Mama said, a few weeks later. "We're going to get a new baby."

"For true, Mama?" Randy beamed. "When?"

As Randy and Mama talked, I saw her wisdom in helping

Randy prepare for becoming a big brother.

I didn't know whether to be embarrassed or not as I told my junior high friends that Mama was pregnant. They all got a big kick out of the news. And Mama was the talk of our church because, in the `60s, most women were done having their families by the time they were 32.

Because of her age, Mama's doctor put her on a low salt diet, as a precaution against toxemia. That meant no canned vegetables and drinking bottled water because Houston's water was so salty.

No matter what Mama said to us, I knew she did not really want this baby. But she began to pray, "Help me understand why, Lord."

The Lord did just that. After the first trimester, Mama came to me. Her face glowed as she said, "You know, Sandee, God has a reason for bringing this baby into the world. This baby is no accident. I'm just anxious to see what God will do with this little fellow."

Randy and I were put in charge of choosing a name. We figured it was going to be a boy, because the only names we picked out were for boys. Our final choice was Paul Timothy Williams.

Soon after that, Dad came in for a week of rest between meetings. That evening he sat on the couch and pulled Mama close to him. He talked about his preaching crusade planned for the Orient, the Philippines and Iceland. "I can send someone in my place," Dad proposed.

"Oh, Gene, you've planned and worked on this crusade for two years. Finally it has come together. You have to go."

Dad's eyes searched Mama's face before he continued in a quieter tone. "You remember that the crusade will last three months April, May and June. That means I'll be gone when our baby is born."

Mama's hand gently rubbed her abdomen. "Gene, God knew all about the crusade when He gave us this baby." Even as tears rolled down her cheeks, a peaceful smile spread across her face. "If He has arranged it so they both come at the same time, well then . . .."

"But, honey, I want to be with you."

"And I want that, too. But God has called you to go and me to stay. I do not want our baby to keep anyone from being saved. This baby needs to add to the kingdom of the Lord, not take away. So you must go."

Everyone held their breath as Mama's courage showed through.

Then Mama's giggle broke the tension after a few moments. "Remember what the doctor said? There isn't anything more that you can do. You've already done your part. To have this baby, we only need me and the doctor."

So it was decided that Dad would keep his overseas commitment.

Later, as I lay in bed, the scene between Mama and Dad kept replaying in my head. I knew my dad. He really meant the offer to cancel his part in this far away crusade. And Mama: saying Dad should go that she wanted him to go. Wow!

Would I have been able to tell my husband it was all right for him to be on the other side of the world when our baby was born?

I couldn't help but smile as I snuggled against my pillow, knowing Mama and Dad loved each other that much, but loved God more. Somehow, my world felt very secure.

It was a good thing my parents were so considerate with each other and in their relationship with God. As word traveled about their decision, we were dismayed at the censure that came from fellow Christians.

"So Gene will not be here when the baby's born? Surely he could be, if he really wanted to."

And: "Dottie, aren't you afraid, at your age, that something will go wrong? Gene is going to cancel his trip, isn't he?"

Mama and Dad remained resolute, despite the criticism. Ma
ma
just made sure everyone understood that it was her decision that Dad go. When God had already proved Himself faithful to them, why would they not trust Him with Dad's around-the-world-in-8
0- days' trip?

One Sunday morning after Dad left, as Mama sat between Randy and me in the balcony of First Baptist Church, she looked at me kind of funny. "Quit that," she whispered. I thought, *What in the world is she talking about?* I sat real still.

A few minutes later, Mama leaned toward my ear. "Sandra, please stop punching me. You're making me nauseated."

"Mama, I haven't touched you."

Just then a bulge formed right below Mama's ribs. A little foot or fist poked once, then again. Mama patted my hand and smiled. "I'm sorry. Your baby brother's at it again."

A few days later Mama, Randy and I were out mowing the yard and pulling weeds. It was such a nice day that Randy and I kept losing interest in our work. Off we'd go in a game of tag. Over and over, Mama insisted that we get the yard done right then. What she didn't tell us then was that her water broke somewhere in the process of our yard work.

When the time came, Mama planned that Mammaw Miller and her best friend Lois would come and stay with her. She knew that Lois would be the calm one.

Mama waited until the yard was finished and then called Mammaw. "Why don't you and Lois come and spend the night?" They came, even though Mama didn't mention that labor was near.

About four o'clock the next morning, Mama's voice broke through my sleep. She was fully dressed. "Sandee, wake up."

I sat up in bed as Mama grabbed my desk in pain. I'd been through this before, so I knew what was happening this time. As the pain eased, Mama said, "We're going to have our baby today."

Randy, still in his pajamas, walked out to the car almost in his sleep. Mammaw sat in the back with us and Mama got into the front seat so Lois could drive to Hermann Hospital. On the way, Randy and I were dropped off at Sampaw's.

We jumped out of the back seat and kissed Mama goodbye. As they pulled out of the driveway, I couldn't help noticing Mama rubbing her abdomen with her eyes closed.

Sampaw opened his front door and Randy went in and right

to bed. Feeling excitement and fear all mixed together, I ran to the window, wondering if Dad knew our baby was on the way.

I later learned that after dropping me and Randy off at Sampaw's, Mama told Lois, "We need to hurry."

Lois ordered, "Don't you dare have this baby in the car."

"Then you'd better step on it," Mama said.

Mama told me later that when she was wheeled on a stretcher out of the delivery room her first thought was to place a call to Dad from the phone in the hall.

"Operator, can you help me place a call to Baguio City, Philippines?"

"Who is this call for?" quizzed the operator.

"Dr. Gene Williams." The phone was so silent that it seemed as if the connection had broken. Mama looked around and saw five nurses surrounding the stretcher, all with handkerchiefs and boo-hooing.

It was night time in the Philippines. Dad's voice broke through the silence. "Hello."

"Gene, we have a baby boy. He was born at seven thirty this morning, and weighs seven pounds five ounces, and he looks just like you."

"Are you okay?" Dad asked in concern.

"I'm just fine."

"What about the baby?"

"He's just beautiful and he's got all of his equipment."

"Well, I love you very much. I wish I were there."

"I love you, too." The nurses' sobs crescendoed.

We learned later that Dad was so excited after Mama's call that he hung up the phone, dressed in a hurry, and took to the street. "Hey, I just got word that my wife had a baby," he told everybody within hearing distance. "A fine new son. Paul Timothy Williams." Most of the strangers didn't even understand English, but they smiled a lot in return.

Monday morning before school, I handed Mammaw Miller a sealed note to take to Mama during visiting hours. We had this running joke in the family that if you went to stay at Mammaw Miller's house, all you got to eat was ham sandwiches and shoestring potatoes. I teasingly wrote in the note to Mama about the ham sandwiches that we were indeed eating, but assured her that we were all right.

When Mammaw picked me up from school that afternoon, Randy was already in the car. Before I opened the door, I saw his big eyes and knew Mammaw was upset. No one said a word on the way home.

Once home, Mammaw climbed out of the driver's seat, slammed the door and marched inside. Randy and I followed her into the house, but at a safe distance. "I know how to cook food," Mammaw muttered as she rushed to the kitchen, slamming pots and pans.

Randy pulled me off to the side and said, "Who set her off?" Then he looked at me and said, "What did you do?"

Mammaw hollered through the house, "Dinner is served."

She slammed a platter of steaks onto the already set table. "I know how to cook food," she repeated as broccoli and baked potatoes joined the steaks. "I always cook dinner."

Uh oh, I thought, *she read my note to Mama*. I felt betrayed that she had invaded my and Mama's privacy.

"Sandra, you should never have bothered your mother with such lies while she was having this baby." Mammaw's face seemed frozen in a frown. Randy and I stole a glance at each other, then started eating. In spite of her scolding, this was the best meal we'd had. Thank goodness, because the next day we were back to ham sandwiches and shoestring potatoes.

Mammaw cooled down. That night she took me to the hospital and sneaked me in to see my mama. Just before entering the hospital room, Mammaw bent down and got in my face. "Don't you dare tell your mother about that awful note."

Needless to say, Mama never received the note. Mammaw Miller kept it until one night when I was twenty. She brought out the note and grandly tore it up before me, saying, "Sandra, I forgive you."

Thankfully, it was Mammaw Fiew who came to help Mama, as she had when Randy and I were born. Together we vacuumed, dusted and did laundry in preparation for Tim's homecoming.

After school Thursday, Randy and I rushed home because Mama and Tim had just arrived. Mama greeted us at the door, with hugs and kisses. "Where is he?" Randy asked. "Can we wake him up and play with him?"

"Sure," Mama smiled. After about 45 minutes, Randy and I had had enough of this baby stuff and ran out to play. With Mama home, we knew all was well.

From the beginning, the only time Tim cried was when he woke up hungry. I loved to touch his soft, pink skin and feel his tiny fingers close around mine.

Randy, now eight, played Little League baseball. Several months before, Dad rigged up a rubber ball on a rope outside for batting practice. Mama had helped Randy with that and played catch when Dad was gone. Now, Randy turned whatever he held in his hands into an imaginary baseball. He'd pick a spot on the wall and hurl one pair of balled-up socks after another at it. When he finished baseball, he played basketball. This was all done in the den, of course. Usually Mama didn't let that bother her but, with a new baby in the house, her patience wore a little thin.

"Mama," I heard her say to Mammaw Fiew, after a couple of days home. "If you really want to help me, let Randy play basketball at your house for a few days. Sandee and I can get us organized while you're gone." Of course, Mammaw agreed. Randy was elated when Pawpaw Fiew came to get him and Mammaw.

Mama and I worked out a routine for the baby's care. In my best big sister fashion, I helped feed, burp and diaper Tim. In the process I learned that babies throw up on you and create the messiest diapers in the world. It wasn't much fun cleaning Tim up, just before having to make lunch for me and Mama.

While Tim slept, Mama often napped. She grew stronger each day. After about a week we couldn't wait for Randy's return.

From the time we were tiny tots, Mama saw that Randy and I had assigned chores. They started small like turning off a light or emptying a wastebasket and grew as we did. So it was no problem now for us to make our beds and help keep the house picked up.

Mama showed us on a world map all the places where Dad was preaching. Finally, he had only Greenland and Iceland left before heading home. We were counting the days.

"Let's go, kids." Mama said on the big day. She straightened Tim's white sailor suit as I shouldered the diaper bag. "Daddy's plane will be in soon," she sang to Tim. Randy helped with the door as we headed for the car.

At Houston's Hobby Airport, Tim snoozed in Mama's arms as we found the place she and Dad had agreed to meet. Just when I thought I couldn't wait another minute to see my dad, he descended the stairs from the plane to walk across the tarmac. "Look, Mama!" My words ran together as I started waving. "Randy, here comes Daddy."

"Daddy?" Randy called and waved. "Daddy?"

"Yeah, Sandee," Mama agreed, smiling. "There's that big ol' handsome fellow of ours."

With a smile stretched all across his face, Dad waved back. His eyes held on Mama as he walked closer.

"Hey, you guys, I've missed you." Dad set his briefcase down before hugging me and pulling Randy close. "My, how you've both grown." Then Dad turned to kiss Mama. "Hello, darling. You look great."

"Oh, I'm so glad you're home, Gene." Mama's free arm closed around Dad's neck. Then she shifted the baby in her arms. "Would you like to meet your son?"

"Hello, little buddy." Dad stroked Tim's cheek as his gaze swept over our new baby. He knew Tim could wait until we were home, so he focused his attention on Randy and me.

It was after our bedtime that Mama and Dad focused on each other and Dad got acquainted with Tim. Our family was complete again for the first time in three months.

Chapter Eight

Mama as Our Teacher

DAD CAME HOME TO A SUMMER BOOKED with meetings in the good old U.S.A. Unwilling to be separated again so soon, he and Mama decided to pack up the little tent trailer and us three kids. We would camp while Dad fulfilled his preaching commitments. "Oh, Sandee." Mama's eyes lit with excitement as she saw another opportunity ahead. "Won't this be a great summer?"

"Are you really taking a six-week-old baby camping?" friends began to ask. "And staying in parks? For the entire summer?"

These were the same friends who thought Dad should have canceled his trip to be home when Tim was born. Now they thought Mama had lost her good sense for sure.

Over Dad's week of rest, he reviewed the summer's schedule and studied in preparation for preaching. Randy and I helped as Mama organized and packed our clothes. We gathered up and checked camping equipment for wear, then added Monopoly and checkers for rainy days. Of course, Randy's baseball and glove would ride beside him on the seat. For Tim's benefit, we included a small plastic tub for bathing, formula for mixing and a just-on-the-market electric bottle sterilizer. An Infant Seat and portable crib completed our camping supplies.

Finally, with itinerary, maps and mileage charts in hand, we set forth on the big trip.

As we came into each town where Dad had a meeting scheduled, we located the nearest camping park. Once camp was set up, Mama unpacked Dad's suits and shirts and checked for wrinkles. Dad then located the pastor and began the visits and prayer times that preceded the meetings. Often some of the church families invited all of us to a meal. Mama and the women talked while Randy and I played with their children. Each night, we went to worship service with Dad.

Wherever we were, Tim woke up each morning with a smile that was contagious. As we drove, he slept to the purr of the motor. Only once was Tim a real problem and that wasn't his fault.

We were somewhere near Shreveport, Louisiana. The church sponsoring Dad's meeting provided our family with a little tin-roofed cottage in the back yard of a wealthy church family for our stay. Most nights, we could stretch out and stay cool enough to sleep. But one night, the hot day's humid air lay trapped inside the house and nothing we did helped cool the house. We were all hot, tired and grumpy.

"My sweet baby," Mama cooed as sweat ran down Tim's chest and usually happy face. His red skin glowed like a lobster's. Whether Mama held Tim or laid him down, he fussed. I tried a lullaby. Randy made funny faces, nothing helped.

"Sandee," Mama commanded, eyes wide with a new idea. She handed me one of Tim's blankets. "Go run some cold water over this, wring it out and bring it back to me."

While Dad held Tim, Mama poured some chilled creme soda pop into one of Tim's bottles. Then she placed the wet blanket in the middle of the floor where the coolest air was and lay Tim on it. She asked me to lift his head slightly and give him the cold creme soda.

"Mercy, Dottie," Dad exclaimed, you're going to kill that boy. Randy and I looked at each other, wondering at Dad's remark.

"Now, Gene," Mama returned, "if Sandra could have chocolate milkshakes when she was six weeks old, a little cream soda won't hurt this baby. Besides he's burning up." Mama's confidence soothed Dad's worry. Between the cool blanket and drink, Tim's redness soon faded. Thank God, he dozed off, so we could, too.

The rest of the summer whizzed by as we criss-crossed the

country for Dad's meetings.

Fall brought school and a return to the old routine. Dad starting coming in and out of our lives again. A week or two on the road, then a few days home.

At two a.m. in early October, Mama heard a knock on the front door. She wasn't sure that she could make it out of the bed, much less to the front door. She held the wall as she walked down the hall. Twisting the door knob that unlocked the door, she turned on the outside light and looked through the locked screen door. To her amazement, Dad was standing on the front porch. He was not supposed to arrive until the following afternoon, but felt impressed to come home early from his meeting. She opened the door and fell in his arms. "Gene, honey, I'm in trouble."

Dad recognized immediately that something terrible was wrong. Her left arm and hand had drawn up. When he got her to the bedroom, he saw where she had thrown up everywhere. Dad spent the rest of the night massaging wherever Mama felt pain. Neither had any idea how serious the situation was. Not until days later, when Mama saw Dr. Bing, did we realize that Mama had suffered a stroke. This altered our lives, especially Mama's and mine.

Mama was unable to take proper care of her four-month-old baby. She quickly taught me at age twelve how to fill her shoes. I became chief cook and bottle washer.

A great host of people were praying for my dear Mama. Within six weeks she improved, but it was almost three years before she was running on all cylinders.

Having to care for Mama and the house caused me to grow and mature very quickly. But the nicest thing about it was that Mama took this as an opportunity to teach me to be self sustaining. She taught me how to be a mama to a baby as she was being a mama to me.

Peppermill was a quiet street and neighborhood kids played together in the park. Tim, big for his age, started playing outside with minimal supervision when he was about three years old. His best friend was Jimmy Hatfield. The family on the corner had the toughies of our street. Mama loved to tell about the day Tim learned how to handle a bully named Sammy.

"What's the matter?" Mama said, opening the door at the sound of Tim's cries.

"Sammy hit me." Tim's fists smeared tears across his face. "They won't let me play."

"Do you want to play?"

"Yeah, Mama," Tim sobbed. "I want to play."

"Haven't you wrestled and fought around with your brother?" Mama's tone remained calm. "Don't you know how to fight?"

"Yes, I know how to fight," Tim insisted. By now, Tim's eyes were dry.

"Well, you go back down there. Don't you hit any of them, but if they hit you, you tear their heads off."

With that, Tim charged back out to the street.

Now Mama wanted Tim to fight his own battles, but she also wanted to be sure he was safe. Mama said later that she remembered when I was about three years old and some older seminary brats gave me some candy that was really jalapeno peppers. My mouth and throat were seriously burned and I was a sick little girl for a while. Not wanting anything like that to happen to Tim, she slipped outside and ducked behind some bushes to watch.

Just then, Dad's car pulled up in the driveway. "What on earth are you doing, Dorothy?"

"Shhhh! Get down here," she whispered, as she pulled on his coat to get him to crouch down behind the bushes.

"What are you doing?" Dad pressed.

"It's Tim. I sent him out to fight his own battle with Sammy, and I'm hiding in the bushes to make sure he's safe."

As Dad spotted Tim, he said, "Dottie, you're going to get that boy killed. . .."

Sammy made a face and yelled at Tim.

Tim put his hands on his hips, looked Sammy in the eye and said, "Boy, if you bother me, I'll knock your head off." Tim's buddy, Jimmy Hatfield, gaped in stunned silence with eyes as big as saucers.

Sammy swallowed hard. He took a step backwards, eyes steady on Tim. Then, without another word, they started playing again. Mama and Dad choked back their laughter. After a few minutes they slipped inside the house, satisfied that Tim was safe and knowing that no lecture could have taught Tim any better.

Just like when it was my turn for new shoes. Mama and I did some window shopping, so we'd know what was available.

"Oh look, Mama." I pointed out a pair of psychedelic, platform shoes like several of my friends had.

"Those are cute, Sandee, but I'm afraid they'll not be in style very long. We can only afford one pair, so you need to be sure they're what you want. These penny loafers might be more practical."

"I really like the others, Mama."

"Well, you think about it. We'll come back next week and buy the ones you've decided on."

I thought about it.

I decided.

When the shoe buying day arrived, Mama and I walked into the store. "May I help you?" the salesman offered.

"Yes," I nodded, as Mama sat down beside me. "I'd like some brown penny loafers, size seven, please."

The salesman eased my feet into the shoes, then slid his stool back so I could walk around. "How do those feel?"

"These shoes feel great." I walked toward the mirror. "I'll take them."

"You know," the salesman turned toward Mama, as he walked us toward the counter. "I see a lot of mothers and daughters who come in to buy shoes and argue the whole time. I'd like to compliment the two of you on how easily you did this."

"Thank you," Mama said, putting her change away.

Mama and I didn't dare look at each other. But as soon as we closed the car doors, we burst out giggling. God had blessed Mama with a wisdom about our uncoupling process. Mama had been willing for me to make the less appropriate decision and learn from it. Or to make the more correct decision and come out ahead. Mama knew I was going to have to make many decisions in life and she was providing me with an umbrella of safety for practice.

Not long after that, Mama gave me an unplanned review of good manners when we went out to the shopping center. Her Sears catalog order was due in and Mama needed just a minute to run in and pick it up. For some reason, the spaces on the side of Sears were extra long like for buses or RVs. Parking was at a premium, but we spotted a couple getting into a car near the store's door. Mama hurried our white Ford station wagon up near their car and flipped on her left turn signal, to await their departure.

Just as Mama began to move forward, a little green VW bug came from the opposite direction, cut in front of her and took the space. Disbelief registered on Mama's face.

A man in his mid-twenties stepped out of the VW, laughing. "Lady, it seems like you're just too slow."

With that, Mama smiled broadly and pulled into the same space, blocking him in. Laughter died as the guy stood with his mouth hanging open.

Mama's smile glistened as she got out of our car, locked it and brushed her hands in the face of the stunned young man. "Isn't it wonderful that there's room for both of us?"

"You can't do that, lady," the young man retorted.

"I just did," she said, strolling toward the store's door. Once inside, I glanced back and saw the man standing in the middle of the parking lot just as he threw down his keys in rage.

We knew our errand was short and the station wagon would be gone long before this fellow was ready to leave. But he didn't know that. Hopefully, Mama taught him that day that it's not nice to steal another person's parking space.

Randy benefited from some of Mama's lessons also. All the boys at Hollibrook Elementary would hang around after school and ride their skateboards in the open air halls. One day Randy went to Mama and said, "Mama, can I get a skateboard? All the guys have one."

"How much do they cost, honey?"

"About forty dollars, or so."

"Well, we can't afford to get it right now, but I'll see what I can do." Mama always loved a challenge and so she took this as one. She began to save five-to-ten dollars every month from the food allowance. And within six months, she had the money for the skateboard. Randy came home from school and Mama said, "There's something in your room you might want to check out."

Randy entered his room and cast his eyes on a brand new, beautiful skateboard. Yet this was a bittersweet moment. Skateboards were no longer in vogue with his buddies. But how was he going to tell Mama? He knew she had saved for six months to get him something that he really wanted. Randy knew this had been a sacrifice for her. What was he to do?

Randy remained silent about his dilemma as he went to give the board a try. To his amazement, a wheel fell off. With a sad face, he brought the board back to Mama.

"I guess we'll just have to go back to the store and get this fixed," Mama quickly comforted.

"Uh. . . uh. Could we trade it in on a football helmet?"

"Well, sure, we can trade it in on anything you want."

The skateboard was only an evidence of Mama's love for Randy. Her sacrifice of love was not lost. Randy was so worried that Mama's feelings would be hurt that he never ever told her skateboarding was no longer popular with the guys. But, I suspect she knew.

Chapter Nine

Mama and Our Growing Pains

AS A CHILD, I WOULD "PLAY THE PIANO" on the dashboard or the back of the car's front seat every time I got in the car. When I was three years old, I sang my first concert at Mammaw Miller's church. That Sunday evening, I sang one chorus after another. Still they asked for more. Mama began to worry that I was running out of choruses to sing when the pastor asked, "Sandee, just sing one more for us?"

I stood there, trying to figure out what other song I knew. Mama held her breath, because she could tell from my expression that we were in trouble. Then I reared back and let'er rip. "Dance with me, Henry . . . Oh, no, baby . . .."

Mama graciously rescued me from an embarrassing situation as she whisked me off to the back of the church.

I really didn't do much with my music until I was a high school junior. One day I walked by the music suite and, just on impulse, said to Miss Cox, the music teacher, "How do you get into the choir?"

"Well, do you want to audition?" she responded.

"Well, I guess so."

After Miss Cox had me sing *My Country 'Tis Of Thee*, I was in the choir.

During the first week of school, Miss Cox asked, "Who would like to audition for All State choir?"

Well heavens, I thought, *I sang* My Country 'Tis of Thee *and made it into this choir. Why not audition for All-State Choir? By the way, what is All State Choir?* As I raised my hand, Miss Cox looked at me as if I had lost my mind.

I excitedly explained to Mama that I was going to audition

for All State Choir. Mama asked, "What is All State Choir?"

"I don't know, but I'm going to audition for it. What do you think?"

"I think it's great. I know you'll do the best you can do." I went to the auditions and to Miss Cox's utter amazement, I became a candidate for All State Choir. This automatically placed me in the All Region Choir and gave me an opportunity in three months to audition for a chair in the All State Choir.

Now came the real challenge. Besides the fact that I could not read music, the songs for All State were written in Latin and Italian. I knew neither language. Aware of my inexperience, Miss Cox chose to help the other candidates in their preparation more than she was willing to help me.

Do I really have what it takes? questioned Mrs. Grouch's former third grade student. Inside I could hear the voice of Mrs. Grouch saying, "You're retarded."

Downhearted, I talked to Mama again. "Sandee, we know your voice is good enough, you just need help with the rest of it. If you really want to go to All State, why don't you see if your old piano teacher will record your part on a tape recorder."

And indeed she did. Since I didn't know enough about music to rely on my skill, I learned the foreign languages and notes by rote memory. Winding and rewinding our reel-to-reel tape recorder for hours, I rehearsed each song until the entire family could sing Mozart's *Requiem Mass* in full.

Finally, the big night came. "Now, Lord," Mama prayed before I left home, "You know how hard Sandee has worked to prepare for this night, but her goal is to honor you. Please keep her voice true and her memory good. We leave the results to You. Amen."

Amen.

When it was over, I could hardly believe the results. Not only had I made All State Choir, but I was awarded first chair. I thought Miss Cox was going to faint. Miss Cox's least likely student had achieved beyond expectation. As she was driving me home that night, Miss Cox humbly apologized. "Sandee, I want you to know that I am sorry. I really had no idea how talented you are. I realize that I did not help you very much. I should have been there for you, too. You were the only student of mine who made All State Choir, and you did it all on your own."

"That's okay, Miss Cox. I just thank you for the opportunity." Then I jumped out of the car and hit the front door. Mama and I jumped up and down in the foyer of the house, squealing with excitement over my good news.

Music appealed to me more and more. During my senior year as I thought about college, I was drawn to music education. Offers for vocal scholarships started coming after I made All State Choir again. *Should I accept the offer from Baylor or Houston Baptist College*? It was a difficult decision, but I decided on Houston Baptist.

The fall of 1969 was a momentous time for Mama. Not only did I enter college, but Tim started first grade.

Mama always said she didn't want her children to be carbon copies of one another. It distressed her when the cookie cutter schools tried to fit all children into one little mold. Yet, it became apparent Tim was like me in one way. His classmates called him stupid, dumb and retarded when he, too, had trouble reading. Mama, ever watchful, suspected a problem early on and tests were scheduled. Each step she took with Tim made me thankful again for all her help to me.

The EEG, or brainwave test, was a frightening experience for Tim. The technician did not explain why she placed wires all over Tim's head, even though Mama asked her to. And she commanded Mama to leave saying, "I work with these little dummies all the time. He'll be all right."

"Mama," Tim asked, on the way home, "What is wrong with my brain?"

"We don't know, honey." Mama's plain truth principle was in action. "That's why we had the test done. This lady—the technician—didn't do her job very well. She should have explained things to you as she went along." Mama sighed. "Tim, I'm sorry, but sometimes in life you run into a nut, and you just met one."

Meanwhile, my college studies introduced me to the relatively new field of learning disabilities. Finally, educators were going to stop applying the label of retarded to every child with a problem. Dyslexia was the disability that got my attention. It sounded just like me and it also sounded just like Tim. I suggested to Mama that she have him tested for this.

When Tim's diagnosis came back "dyslexia," Mama had a running start on how to help. Each afternoon, Mama took a nap so she would be fresh and able to work with Tim after school to improve his reading skill.

As Tim started second grade, Mama remembered my problems and didn't want a repeat. Therefore, she made what became her first annual speech to Tim's teachers. "I have brought you an emotionally stable child. He's dyslexic, but he is not dumb. I realize you are educated enough to know this, too. So, don't send me back a child who is unhappy."

Then early in the fall, Tim fell while playing touch football with some children and was in terrible pain. We rushed him to the emergency room. Mama listened closely as Dr. Bing described Tim's badly fractured right femur (thigh bone) and the required treatment. Tim was to be in the hospital for six-weeks of traction before a cast could be put on. Seeing Tim hurt was bad enough, but Mama also remembered that Tim was the only one in our family not covered by insurance. She went to phone Dad—who was in a meeting — with the news.

"Now, honey," Dad said, trying to reassure her. "Boys do things like that. Just don't be upset about it. Let's praise the Lord he wasn't hurt more."

"Yeah, Gene, but he's got to be in the hospital."

"Well, praise the Lord." Dad calmly said.

"For six weeks," Mama explained. Dad's gasp on the other end of the line let her know he understood the physical and financial aspects of Tim's injury.

This time, there was a brief pause before Dad said, "Praise the Lord anyway."

Tim was placed in traction and had to depend on others to help with his basic needs. Nurses were in and out of his semi-private room, but Mama gave Tim all his care and kept his room neat. When Mammaw Miller or one of us could relieve her,

Mama came home just long enough to freshen up.

But one day something came up that Mama had to leave Tim for about an hour without a family member there. Of course, she told the nurses that she would be gone and for how long. She told us later what she found when she returned.

"I'm back, Tim," Mama said, turning into Tim's room. Her eyes fixed on Tim's over-bed table, where his urinal had been left touching his water pitcher. A washcloth, obviously soiled during a bedpan episode, lay beside it. "Did someone help you with the bedpan, Tim?"

"Yes, Mama. One of the nurses came in."

"Well, I need to talk to her." With that, Mama drew herself up to full height and marched down to the nurses' station.

"I told you I was leaving for a short time and my son was in your care until I returned." She now had the attention of several doctors as well as the nurses. "You do not even have to touch Tim when I'm here—I wait on him hand and foot. Now, after less than an hour away, I return and find him in this condition. There is no excuse. Don't you ever let me find him this way again."

Mama marched back to Tim's room. Several staff members followed. In no time, the room was straight and Tim's water pitcher had been replaced.

Mama never did get used to other parents placing their children in the hospital and only checking on them once a day. Perhaps it was the correct way for other parents, but Mama would never traumatize her child that way. She thought that Tim's physical discomfort was all he should have to handle.

When the school arranged teachers for Tim, Mama studied his situation. She knew it would be hard for Tim to concentrate with another child-patient in the room. Spotting an alcove down the hall, Mama approached Tim's nurses.

"When the teachers come to work with Tim," Mama shared her plan, "they'll need a quiet place for study. I'd like you to roll Tim, in his bed, down to the alcove for his school time."

"No, indeed," came the response. "We cannot do that."

"If you can't do it," Mama's determination showed again,

"I'll do it. But it is going to be done."

A couple of days later, Mama maneuvered Tim's bed—traction and all—toward the door of his room. The teacher was due in a few minutes. Suddenly, two nurse aides appeared and helped roll the bed into the alcove. Nothing was said about their change of mind. Each lesson day after that, Tim and his bed traveled the hallway before and after school time.

As teenagers, Randy and I gained a lot of experience by the time Tim's six weeks in the hospital were up. Mama had always been there for us, now we could be there for her. We bought food, cooked meals, did laundry and took care of the house. And, Dad was always available by phone even if he wasn't at home.

Before Tim's discharge, he got a body cast which left his chest, arms, head and toes showing. A rod anchored between his legs made turning and handling him easier. We were all glad to have them back home. Months of care and work lay ahead to get Tim back on his feet.

A week or so later, Dad took Randy and me to a junkyard. While Dad conducted his business, Randy and I spotted some ponies near the back of the yard. "Dad," Randy said, as we raced back to the office, "come see what we've found to help Tim get better."

Dad looked them over, then turned to the owner. "How much are your ponies?"

"Twenty-five dollars."

"Well," Dad paused just a moment. "Y'all pick one out."

Randy and I settled on one that reminded me of the little red pony. He was perfectly shaped, like a miniature red horse with a cream mane and tail. Dad arranged for the pony's delivery to our house, then we headed home.

I'm not sure when Dad told Mama. After all, most people would get a dog, but here we were with a pony. But she joined us to watch Tim's face light up when he saw his pony go into our backyard. Tim named him Little Chief.

After that, Tim's bed was placed in front of the sliding glass door. Little Chief would find his way up the covered patio, nose right up and look at Tim, just like he knew his job was to cheer up this little fellow. Sometimes Mama slid the door open so Tim could rub Little Chief's nose or feed him an apple. Tim's desire to get well grew everyday. He wanted to ride Little Chief more than anything else.

Tim's schooling continued. His teacher came to the house three days a week, and Mama worked with him the other days. Eighteen months after his diagnosis, Tim could do a series of tasks in order. Quite an accomplishment for a dyslexic kid whose letters and words get all jumbled up. He'd be the first to tell you, without Mama's help and support, it wouldn't have happened.

Finally Tim's cast was cut off. Mama and Dr. Bing stood watching Tim practice using crutches in the office hallway.

"When I come back, Doc," Tim promised, "I'll be walking."

At home, "I want to walk" became Tim's motto. His character and determination showed when pain filled his eyes with tears. But Tim didn't stop trying. When the hurting got too bad, Mama ran a bathtub full of warm water to ease Tim's pain. Riding Little Chief seemed to help the most.

"Well, bless your heart, Tim." Dr. Bing's grin split his face, as Tim strode down the hall at his next visit. Shaking his head in amazement, the doctor said, "You did it, didn't you?"

Soon after that, one of the neighbor kids climbed our fence and spotted Little Chief. Adults overheard the kids talking about a pony in our backyard, and someone reported us to the authorities. At least Tim was back on his feet before we had to board Little Chief elsewhere.

If nothing else, Mama got better at her parenting. It was like she was a mama bear with her baby cubs, willing to turn loose at the right time, but nobody had better hurt them.

As for the $2,000 hospital bill, God continued to do His stuff. Dad simply included the need in his monthly newsletter, and there was an outpouring of gifts from many supporters. The total of the money given met the $2,000 need, to the penny.

Well, praise the Lord.

While Tim was recuperating, I was enjoying my first year at college. The only requirement of my scholarship was that I be a member of the Houston Baptist College Singers. New outfits, chosen by the director, were ordered from Europe. Mama went with me to a fitting one Saturday. When I gave the little black lady my name, she brought out a white see-through pants suit. Neither Mama nor I said anything, but my heart sank as I slipped into it.

There's no way I can wear this thing. It leaves nothing to the imagination.

When I stepped out to let Mama view this lovely creation, she drew a breath trying to remain calm. "Well, Sandee," Mama said, once the lady began fitting my outfit. "I didn't expect you to wear something like this for Houston Baptist."

"Do you mean," the fitter said, before I could answer, "these are for Houston Baptist College?"

"Yes, ma'am," Mama affirmed, shaking her head. "They are."

"Pshaw!" The lady's animated face drew up in a frown. "I thought they were for a dance band."

Whatever the consequences, I knew I could not wear this outfit. Pants suit in hand, I headed for the director of the singers, to let him know. I was told that I absolutely had no choice. I had to wear this outfit if I was going to remain in the Houston Baptist College Singers.

"I can't believe," Mama said, once we were in the car, "that a Christian college is asking my daughter to wear something provocative and suggestive."

"Those outfits are just awful, Mama." With that, our tears overflowed. Both of us were wishing Dad was home instead of overseas in a crusade. We needed his wisdom.

"Sandee," Mama said, as we continued heading home. "I cannot let this go by. If the school makes you wear these uniforms, every Baptist in Texas is going to know about it."

Once home, Mama notified a wealthy friend about the situation. Since some people at the college had already belittled my walk with the Lord and called Mama and Dad my "apostolic parents," Mama was not sure she would be listened to. This man was on the advisory committee to the college president. He would be heard.

Mama knew the president of the Houston Baptist Pastors' Conference. She called him and explained what had happened, then asked, "May we come model one of these uniforms?"

"Yes, you may." A time was set for the next Monday, at their regular meeting

"Now, I want you to know," Mama added, "that I'm going to call the papers and television stations and have them cover this. Every Baptist in Texas must know about this."

"Thank you for letting me know, Dottie. I'll see you Monday."

Mama frequently breathed a prayer for wisdom as Sunday and its normal church activities passed. My prayers echoed hers. While we didn't know this situation's end, we knew God had it in hand.

Early Monday morning, Mama tried several times to phone her best friend, a fashion designer.

"Where in the world have you been?" Mama demanded, when the friend finally answered about nine o'clock.

"I've been out at Houston Baptist since seven thirty."

"What in the world for?"

"Well, I got a call from the president's office to come look at the singing group's new outfits," Mama's friend sighed. "I've been telling them that those singers' uniforms will not do. And, there's nothing that can be done to salvage them." So the fashion show at the pastor's conference was canceled.

My music professor cornered me the next week. "Sandee, I don't understand why you can't wear these new uniforms."

"I sing all over this city," I said, knowing I must make my point in no uncertain term. "People know what I believe. Those outfits mock my Christian testimony."

"Well," his anger seethed. "The real reason you can't wear them is because your daddy's a preacher."

Thankfully I recalled all the times Mama and Dad had said, "Sandee, these are our convictions. But it's important that you have your own. Look in the Bible for direction and pray about it. We know you'll do the right thing." Never had they used Dad's ministry to keep me from doing anything.

My eyes calmly met his. "In our family, we either do or don't do things because we love the Lord. Dad's being a preacher doesn't have anything to do with it."

The Houston Baptist College Singers soon had another white pants suit. This time it was very thick double knit from Neiman Marcus. It was clear that modesty was the message.

Amazingly my tests weren't finished yet. Remember the go-go dancing days? Well, this same professor had elevated platforms built in order to assign two girls from our group so they could go-go dance while the rest of us sang.

"Well, Mama, you won't believe what happened to me today. I was assigned to one of those 'go-go' spots."

"You're kidding." Mama gasped.

My friends and I laughed all day long. "Mama, do you know, how hard it is to sing and not move a single thing?"

With that, Mama said, "Do you think anything good is going to happen to you down there at that school?"

In fact, many good things did happen to me. I received an excellent education and made many good friends. I have fond memories of my Houston Baptist days. Every conviction was tested while there. As always, Mama was my encourager. As the uncoupling continued, Mama allowed my convictions and my belief system to become my own.

Chapter Ten

Mama as Wife, Mother, Daughter

ONE OF MAMA'S GREATEST JOYS was traveling with Dad. She delighted in telling her experiences when she got home, especially when it meant telling on herself. One of her favorite escapades took place at Miami Beach's Fountaine Blue Hotel, when New Orleans Seminary alumni held their annual breakfast during the Southern Baptist Convention.

The morning of the breakfast, she slipped into her new blue s ilk dress and white spike-heeled shoes—the latest style. Adding a white picture-frame hat with matching gloves and handbag, she felt dressed to the hilt.

Dad's eyes lit up. "Well, Dottie, don't you look nice this morning."

"Thank you." she smiled, thinking, *no one will believe my beautiful outfit came from Houston's very own Bargain Gusher.*

They followed a bell captain's directions and found the room reserved for the seminary breakfast. Dad was still fairly new in evangelism, so besides seeing old friends, they hoped to make additional contacts for meetings.

Friends waved as they entered the lovely room. After greeting them, Dad spotted a table with two empty seats between two couples he and Mama had known in seminary. Several professors completed the ten people who filled their table.

Round tables covered with white linens set off sparkling crystal and silverware. Glasses of orange juice, kept chilled by crushed ice in a silver base, stood at each place setting. As Mama sat down, the table moved slightly, and she realized it had a false top to make it larger.

Mama turned to talk to the man on her left. Mama never

could talk without using her hands, so they were going, too. Out of the corner of her eye, she saw her juice glass move. *Oh, no,* she thought, *I must have bumped it*. Just then, silence filled the room.

Mama made a grab for the glass.

Her hand hit the waiter's with a loud smack. Heads turned. She looked into the waiter's astonished face and gulped. "I'm so sorry . . . I . . .."

Thud! The man on her left dropped the sugar bowl onto the table between Mama and Dad. The unstable top rocked, setting silverware a jingling.

Of course, everyone thought Mama had committed that *faux pas*, as well.

Mama could hold it no longer. Her giggle erupted. Laughter and talk resumed around the room. Thankfully, she finished breakfast without further incident.

The group from the table walked together as they headed for the convention hall. Naturally, Mama kept talking. Dad held the hotel's main door open for her as she stepped out onto the rubber welcome mats. What she didn't notice was the little indented squares that made up the mats. With her next step, she planted her heels in those squares, stumbled forward slightly, and walked right out of her shoes.

Dad looked at her with astonishment. "You know, I just cannot take you anywhere," he chuckled, as he assisted Mama in regaining her composure.

A few years later, in 1968, Dad had meetings scheduled for the Orient, and invited Mama to go along. Mammaw Miller agreed to keep Tim, who was still in elementary school. With relations strained between Mammaw and Randy, he stayed home by himself. He could drive and knew my apartment was less than twenty minutes away.

Dad first preached in the Philippines, then they flew to Vietnam, where the war was at its peak. In Saigon, the Baptist missionaries met Mama and Dad and took them to their hotel. Unknown to the missionaries, this hotel was now a place where American soldiers brought prostitutes. It was not the sort of place Dad usually took Mama. Mama was aghast.

"Dottie," Dad encouraged, "I know parts of this trip are difficult. But, when we get to Hong Kong, you're going to be in the Peninsula Hotel. We've only visited there before, but it's first class, I guarantee. No hookers. Just hang on until we get there."

The missionary ladies in Saigon arranged a tea for Mama the next day. They got their hair done and gussied up all beautiful. During tea, conversation again reminded Mama of where she was. The missionary hostess mentioned a government official who lived next door. That morning, a would-be assassin was caught and killed there, before he could harm the official. Later the missionaries showed Mama and Dad home movies of the recent, fierce Tet offensive. The film indicated that a battle had gone on right in the front porch and yard of the missionaries. After the battle was over, the missionaries had gone out for supplies and the film showed them having to move bodies every few feet. Vietnam was a very sobering experience for Mama.

The Vietnamese Christians kept the windows open in the little one-story church where Dad preached in Vietnam. Across the church front stretched a veranda with built-in benches. Missionaries and American soldiers of all denominations came to the meetings. A common hope of winning the Vietnamese to the Lord was felt.

One night, missionary Jim Humphreys invited a Vietnamese group who were learning English to the service. Mama said it was a beautiful picture to see the Vietnamese fill the veranda's benches and American soldiers on their knees praying while Dad preached. Mama remembered seeing other soldiers cavorting with prostitutes in the hotel. "It just goes to show you," Mama said, "that not all our troops are following the devil."

The missionaries, used to their surroundings, took Mama and Dad to a nice restaurant on the coast. Jim Humphreys drove the unairconditioned Volkswagen van with its slipping clutch.

On their return to Saigon, Jim stopped at a U.S. base commissary. Everyone got back into the VW van with chocolate milkshakes and hot apple pies in hand. As Jim drove, flashes from one mountain to the other identified fire fights between

American soldiers and the Communist Vietcong.

Dear Lord! Mama thought. *What am I doing here?*

Right after they returned to Saigon the very road they had traveled was closed to civilian traffic.

On their arrival in Hong Kong, an appointed delegation warmly welcomed Mama and Dad like visiting royalty at the airport. Now, Mama could hardly wait to get to the Peninsula Hotel's comfort. The prospect of having a hot bath, sipping tea in the lovely lobby and being a pampered patron had pulled her through this trip's rough spots.

The Chinese driver headed toward the hotel. Then, without explanation, the car stopped across the street at the YMCA. Next thing Mama and Dad knew, they were checked in at the Y. Of course, not wanting to offend their hosts, they did not question the Chinese.

"You just sit down here," Dad told Mama as soon as they had seen the rickety old twin beds and the greeters had left. "Don't unpack your suitcase or anything. There's been a foul-up. I'm going across the street and talk to the head of the hotel."

Mama followed Dad's instructions.

The hotel manager smiled at the sight of Dad. "Dr. Williams, I am so sorry. I had your reservation and was expecting you. Then your friends here in Hong Kong canceled it. So sorry, there are no rooms available now. If I had anything, I'd give it to you."

"Honey," Dad reported back. "I'm very disappointed. I can't explain this." By now, Mama was shedding a few tears. "I don't know any way we an handle it without offending the Chinese," Dad continued. "It looks like we're going to have to stay here."

"Gene," Mama said through tears and sobs. "I'm going to sleep at the YMCA, but I want you to know that I'm <u>staying</u> at the Peninsula."

"That's all right, Dottie," Dad comforted, knowing what a good sport Mama had been all this trip. "That's what I promised you could do."

So she and Dad had Eggs Benedict for breakfast every morning in the Peninsula's dining room which overlooked the bay. She got her hair done and had afternoon tea at the Peninsula.

They never did learn why their reservations at the Peninsula were canceled.

Dad's next stop was Japan.

"Look, Gene," Mama motioned to a group of Japanese whose arms were filled with flowers and small gifts. "See those people gathered over there? I wonder who they are here to welcome."

"Honey," Dad smiled, recognizing Dr. Watanabe. "I think they're here to welcome us."

Mama loved Dad so much, it was always a joy for her to see how much the people he ministered to loved him, also. Most of all Mama loved the fact that Dad allowed God to use him in such unusual ways. "It's amazing," Mama often remarked to us kids, "what God does through your father."

On one occasion, Mama and Dad boarded a plane, on the way to Dad's upcoming revival. Just after Mama started down the aisle, someone stepped out in front of Dad, blocking his way.

Mama walked on toward the plane's mid-section. As she neared her exit-row seat, business talk floated to her. Looking around, Mama spotted a half dozen suited yuppies in their three-piece suits.

"I believe, sir," Mama said to the one who was where her ticket said she should be, "that you're sitting in my seat."

"Well, lady," the man abruptly motioned, "there are a whole lot of seats around here. Why don't you take one of those?"

"Sir, my mother didn't raise a dummy, and I feel fairly sure your mother didn't raise a dummy, either." By now, all the yuppies were tuned in. Mama smiled and continued. "If you travel half as much as I do, you know there is more room in the seat where you are sitting. That's the reason my husband and I requested them. Now would you please move?"

Laughter rolled from the other yuppies. Face red, the young man gathered his papers and briefcase to move. Mama settled into her seat.

Just then, Dad appeared. "What's everybody laughing about?"

Mama's face proclaimed innocence, "Oh, nothing much. I

just rescued your seat for you." Then her giggle broke through as she told Dad what had happened.

Mama's ability to laugh at herself pulled her through many times that could have otherwise been disasters. And she always looked for the positive aspects.

We were all aware of how much Mama loved to travel with Dad, but we also knew that she felt her first priority was being with us when we needed her.

Like the time when Randy was in high school and really got her attention while she was whipping potatoes for supper.

"Mama, there's something I need to ask you about."

"Okay, ask me."

"Well, now, I don't want you to misunderstand and think this happens to me everyday. But, uh, what do you do when a girl propositions you?"

Mama turned off the beaters. She wanted to shout her question, but she thought, *This is a time to be very calm. If I want my son to ask me hard questions in the future, I must not act shocked*. "Well," Mama turned toward Randy, and spoke as calmly as possible. "Who's been propositioning you?"

"Several times, when I've come out to my car after football practice, there has been a girl standing there. By my car."

"Well, what did she say?" Mama wasn't real sure Randy knew what a proposition was. Then Randy repeated the girl's words, "I would like to have sex with you," and all Mama's doubts were dispelled.

Yep, that sure is a proposition, she thought.

"I . . . I . . .," Randy struggled for words. "Mama, I'm not real sure that I gave the right answer."

"What did you tell her?"

"Well, I said, 'No, thank you. I don't believe I want to'." Mama said that he searched her face before continuing. "I just don't know whether I said it the right way."

"Randy," Mama's relief made her smile. "I don't know of any better answer than that. I'm very proud of how you handled this situation. And, I'm even more pleased because it is your conviction that is the basis for your answer."

While Randy was still in high school, he pulled me aside one day in the front yard. We'd talked before about his desire to preach, and I'd watched him struggle with it for quite a while. Randy had seen me searching for answers not so long before. Now we talked about the need for confession of sin and yielding to God's will. We agreed to pray as he searched for God's answer.

"That would be wonderful," Mama said when Randy told her what he was pondering. "We would be pleased if you became a preacher, but we'd also be pleased with you if you didn't preach. It has to be God calling you. If you're going to be the preacher you ought to be, you've got to know that God set you apart."

Randy approached Dad as he shaved a few days later. "I need some help. How do I know if preaching is what I want to do, or if God wants me to?"

Dad paused between razor strokes. "Well, Randy, God is so good that sometimes He'll put a desire in our hearts, then reveal to us that it's His will and desire as well."

Dad's answer helped Randy find the peace he needed. Soon he stood before the church, making his decision public.

Then he was invited to preach his first sermon. Dad was away, so Randy asked Mama to help him prepare. As though God stamped his approval on Randy's decision, a lady came forward during the song of invitation to receive Christ.

Mama's rejoicing spilled over in prayer. *God, you gave us our children and we gave them back to you. There's not anything you could have given me, nothing anybody could have done or said or given me, that would bring me more pleasure than this. Thank you, Lord.*

As Randy's high-school graduation neared, Mama's joy truly overflowed one day. "Mrs. Williams," the football coach offered. "I just want you to know that anytime there was a troubled student we couldn't reach, Randy was the one we turned to. Do you know what the students called him?"

"No."

"They called him 'Preach'." Mama smiled as she caught a glimpse of Randy's influence. "And they didn't do that to tease him. It was a term of endearment. We're going to miss him around here," the coach said.

Graduation plans for Randy filled our house with excitement. However, Mammaw Miller was pouring vinegar into our cup of joy. During my college years, she had insisted on giving me sterling silver flatware. As Randy's graduation neared, my flatware gifts increased.

"What do you plan to give Randy for graduation?" I asked Mammaw.

"Nothing. I can't afford another thing. I've already spent too much on this sterling silver for you."

For years when Randy sat next to her on the couch and Tim entered the room, Mammaw Miller had ordered, "Get up, Randy. Get up so my grandson can sit by me." She always gave me and Tim very expensive gifts for Christmas and birthdays but seldom spent much energy or money on gifts for Randy.

Mama, of course, was not blind to all this. She knew how much Mammaw Miller slighted Randy. And it hurt. I could tell it hurt when I looked into Mamma's eyes after such an instance.

Randy was no fool either. He was bright enough to know he was being deliberately snubbed. But, thank goodness, Randy's control was such that he never made a scene.

I was determined that Mammaw Miller was going to give Randy a graduation present, and a good one, too. She, herself, had given me an example of how to deal with such dilemmas. So, for the first time, I stood my ground with Mammaw Miller.

I said it firmly. "Mammaw, you are going to give Randy a graduation present. And not something cheap, either."

She jumped back. "No, I'm not. I'm flat broke."

It infuriated me that she had never liked Randy and showed it. So I reached back into my large bag of experiences with her on how to manipulate people. And I used one of her own tactics.

"But, you <u>can</u> afford it, because I'll take all this silver back." Surprise registered on her face. "Then I'll take the money and buy Randy the biggest graduation present he could ever receive and I'll put your name on it."

Mammaw had been outfoxed and she knew it. She didn't say

the words, "I surrender," but her look showed that I'd beaten her to the draw.

"Well, Mammaw," I followed up, "are you going to get your grandson a graduation present, or do I have to do it for you?"

"You can keep your silverware, Sandee," she grumped. "I'll come up with something."

"Something nice?"

"Uh, huh, nice."

She gave Randy $100. Randy hugged her and said, "Mammaw, that's just what I need."

Mama tossed me a quick smile. She didn't have to say a word. She knew I had something to do with it, even though I'd never told anyone.

While the public's attention was riveted on Watergate, Randy enrolled as a ministerial major at Liberty Baptist College in Lynchburg, Virginia. I graduated from college and signed up for my Master's in music education at Sam Houston State University.

Then, to cap it all off, Dad accepted a professorship in evangelism at Liberty Seminary in Lynchburg, Virginia. Riding herd on household affairs, Mama sold the house and managed the move quite well while Dad was finishing his summer revival schedule.

On a Saturday night during one of the worst snowstorms of the season, Mama got the phone call. Tim, now in junior high, had just gone to bed. Dad and Randy were returning from a short trip when Mama heard from Jacksboro, Texas. Her father, Pawpaw Fiew, had died suddenly of a heart attack.

Pawpaw's oft-repeated words comforted Mama as she recovered from the shock: "When my time comes, I hope God will be gracious enough to just take me. I'd like to just drop dead. I don't want to linger and go through what some of my relatives have."

Mammaw Fiew welcomed us with open arms. "He went the way he wanted to," she sobbed.

Mammaw Fiew grieved. We all did. The funeral was held in their church and we followed the hearse to the cemetery. Dad held onto Mama, who kept a close watch on her mother as the preacher intoned the familiar words while Pawpaw's coffin dropped slowly into the grave.

Mammaw Fiew had a difficult time with losing her childhood sweetheart. Nearly two years went by following Pawpaw's funeral and she was still not herself. She barely left her house, and refused to leave Jacksboro. Mama and I met there to see what could be done.

All of Mama's efforts to coax her mother into a healthier stage of grief were fruitless. She couldn't even get Mammaw Fiew, who before Pawpaw's death had never missed services, to attend her church. The last thing Mama said to Mammaw Fiew before we left was, "Mama, I don't understand this. Daddy's been gone two years. You know he's gone. His body's out there in the graveyard. Is that why you won't leave town?"

Mammaw said nothing, but her tears increased.

"You've been a woman of great faith all of your life. You know Daddy is with the Lord. Yet you're choosing to grieve yourself to death. I really do believe Daddy would be very upset with you for not going on with your life."

Mammaw refused to respond to anything Mama said, but she knew Mama was right.

We left and drove directly to the doctor's office. Mama wanted to talk with Mammaw Fiew's regular physician. "I don't know what she's saying to you," Mama told the doctor, "but she is not okay. She won't leave her house except to come here. And she won't consider leaving this town even for a day. All she does is cry for hours every day."

"We had no idea she was still grieving so much," the doctor said. "She always seemed so chipper here."

"All I know is that my mother's in trouble and I've got to find somebody to help her."

"I'll tell you what we're going to do," the doctor declared. "I'm going to find a reason to call her in so I can talk turkey to her about her depression."

Before Mama left town she also stopped at a phone and called Mammaw's pastor to let him know how serious the situation was. He promised to do everything he could to minister to her. Mama was now convinced that Mammaw had put on a front for all these people.

Sadness overcame Mama on the way home. "Sandee," she said, "I never dreamed I'd have to speak so strongly to my own mother. Outside of your daddy, she's the best friend I ever had." She sniffed into her handkerchief. "Now that the professionals around her know there's a problem, I just pray to God that they can do something about it."

In mid-summer Mammaw Fiew's brother came and picked her up so they could attend a family reunion in Wynnewood, Oklahoma. Mammaw laughed, teased, and had a great time. Mama seemed relieved that maybe Mammaw had turned a corner. Maybe this trip had helped her pull out of her grief.

We learned later that the morning after she returned from Oklahoma, Mammaw Fiew began to have difficulty breathing. Thinking it was an allergy attack, she asked a neighbor to drive her to the doctor's office for a shot.

"Come right on back." The nurse escorted Mammaw Fiew and the neighbor to an exam room. The nurse helped Mammaw Fiew onto the table and put a small pillow under her head. "You lie down, Mrs. Fiew, while I go get the doctor."

Almost as soon as the nurse left the room, the neighbor said she heard a gurgling sound from Mammaw Fiew.

"Nurse?" The neighbor ran to the door. "Doctor?"

Mammaw Fiew was dead before the doctor entered her room. Her supposed allergy attack was really heart failure. Having her lie flat was more than Mammaw Fiew's heart could stand.

Mama received another phone call from Jacksboro.

Randy, Dad and I came in from different directions to meet Mama and Tim in Dallas. We drove to Jacksboro to view the body. There was no sign of stress or struggle on her, because she had died so easily. Mama looked at Mammaw Fiew in her pink dress. "Isn't she the most beautiful thing you've ever seen?"

"No," Randy said, shaking his head. "She's not right. She's just simply not right."

"What's the matter?" I asked. "I don't see anything wrong with her."

"They don't have the right kind of bra on her," Tim said. Mammaw Fiew was well endowed and always wore long-line bras which held her very nicely. "They don't have a bra on her. That's what's wrong with her. She doesn't have a bra on."

"I'll go ask the undertaker," Randy said, before Mama or I could open our mouths.

"The one she was wearing was old and stretched-out," the undertaker explained.

"Well," Randy asked, "if Tim and I went and got a different one, would you put it on her?"

"Yes," the undertaker replied, "of course I would."

"I know exactly where she kept them," Tim said. Off my brothers went as Mama and I stood there looking at each other. We couldn't believe what these boys were saying or doing.

Tim and Randy returned a short time later. The undertaker rolled the casket out and did his part. "Yeah," Tim said when the casket was back in place. "Now she looks right."

"Yep. That's what she needed," Randy added.

Mama and I again looked at each other and quietly snickered. All her family was aware Mammaw Fiew struggled with her heavy bosom, and the resultant backache, all of her life. Mama and I knew two things for sure. Mammaw would have had a fit if she had known what shape her bra was in when she died. And she would have gotten a big kick out of the boys going to all this trouble to make her look right.

Chapter Eleven

Mama and the Family Secret

DURING AMERICA'S BICENTENNIAL YEAR, the opportunity came for Dad to do a weekly evangelistic TV show in Dallas. Mama and he prayed for wisdom about leaving Liberty Seminary and starting this new venture.

With a slow-down of Lynchburg's economy, houses were not selling. As Mama searched for an realtor, she found a just-married young man with personality and hustle. Then, leaving it in God's hands, Mama put their house on the market. Two months later, their house sold when others were still listed after two years. Mama and Dad felt that this confirmed their decision to launch the new venture.

While house hunting in Dallas, Dad ran into an old Baylor buddy. Now in real estate, the man picked up quickly on Mama and Dad's plans. "I've got a place you have to see."

Dad's buddy drove Mama and him by a 5,000-square-foot, Georgian colonial-style house. It looked right out of the popular TV soap, *Dallas*.

Mama gasped in admiration.

Dad's face clouded. "We can't begin to afford anything like that."

Dad's old chum refused to be stymied. "What say, let's take a look inside."

"Yeah," Mama agreed. "Let's go look, Gene."

The house sat on five landscaped acres, with a three-car garage and a circle drive in front. When they went inside, they saw that the rooms were huge. With five bathrooms, it was set up perfectly for Dad to have a private office wing. Behind the house, in a grove of oak trees, was an inground pool and a big horse barn and plenty of spread to run horses.

"And the school system is excellent for your son, Tim," the Baylor alumnus assured.

"What a lovely place," Mama sighed. "But God would have to work a real miracle to put us here."

"Well, now," Dad's friend urged. "I know you like the house, so why don't you pray about it?"

And they did pray. A week or so later, Dad made what he considered a ridiculously low offer of $150,000 for the entire property, knowing that the barn alone was worth $50,000. Interest rates at that time were climbing past twelve percent. Dad asked the seller to hold the loan at six percent. Like our house on Peppermill, the people owned the property outright and accepted Dad's offer. This meant that the monthly house payment was in the $500 range. Our whole family rejoiced again at God's goodness.

Mama's creative bent got a real workout as she helped with sets for *Concern For The World*, Dad's thirty-minute TV program. Again, I saw her live out a "followship" attitude with Dad. The key was Mama's attitude. The issue was not whether or not she was supposed to do this. It was learning to follow and trust God to lead her man in the way He wanted him to go. Then, because she followed, Dad felt secure enough to release her for God's service, without being overpowered by her many talents.

Mom watched network shows and proposed ideas for Dad's production. The crew members shook their heads. "You've got great ideas, Miss Dottie," they said. "We just can't handle them on this show."

"Well," rang her optimistic comeback, "they do it on so-and-so's show. I know we can do it if they can." Of course she didn't mention that so-and-so's show had a million-dollar budget.

The crew caught Mama's enthusiasm.

They liked working with her because Mama was very respectful and gracious to them. But they knew good quality was expected. To please Mama, the set builders tried doing things her way. Soon they were doing creations that they didn't before think possible.

Mama ran the show from the control room, too. Dad and Randy alternated preaching, Tim did the announcing and I sang for each show. It was a real family operation and Mama loved every minute.

Not long after the show began, Mama and Dad said, "Sandee, what would you think about directing a group of singers for the show?"

"Ummm. That could be a pile of fun."

We tossed ideas back and forth until we decided on using young people, ages seventeen to twenty. Dad suggested calling the group "Concern Singers." Mama helped with the auditions, and soon we were on the air.

Mama made good use of people's time by having the featured singer come in one day and tape songs for several successive shows. Mama carefully matched up the background sets, then put the right pieces together for a complete program.

Usually Mama stayed pretty calm during shooting sessions. But one time she nearly lost her cool with the cameramen. It was during my solo shots, and the cameramen insisted on shooting me from the waist up. Because I'm well endowed like my Mammaw Fiew, that angle made my chest look huge.

"Shoot Sandee from the shoulders up," Mama told the cameramen. "Do not shoot her from the waist up."

Their shots did not change.

"Do not shoot Sandee from the chest up," Mama declared, a few takes later. "Shoot from the neck up, or get her whole body."

If they heard, the video tapes did not show it.

Mama tried again. "Do not cut Sandee's shots like that."

When nothing changed this time, Mama decided to really communicate with these men. She stalked out in front of the cameras and asked, "Do any of you guys have a breast fetish?"

Wow! I thought, struggling to keep my face straight. Of course, they knew she was not being ugly. It was just her way of saying, I've asked and asked you to please not do that, and you're still doing it.

Without waiting for an answer, she walked back and sat

down. The camera rolled again. You know what? They never shot me from the waist up or the chest up again. Either my whole body was on camera, or neck up only. The subject never came up after Mama set them straight.

When visitors toured the TV station, they always seemed to make it to our set. Mama's creations for our show were some of the best in the business. I still remember her surprised expression when she was introduced as the producer of *Concern For The World*. She never thought what her title was, she was just pitching in, helping Dad do what was needed.

During the second year of the show, Dr. McCoy suspected Mama might have uterine cancer. The decision was made that she have a hysterectomy. While she was in the hospital, fifteen-year-old Tim wrote her a note. *Mama, I wanted you to know, whatever I am or will be, I could not have been without you. Your help and encouragement have meant so much all through my life. I wanted you to know, in case something happened to you.*

Tim, like Randy and me, counted Mama a dear friend. We were doubly relieved that the pathology report was benign. Not only was our mama okay, but so was our friend.

The TV program aired for a little more than three years. By the time 1979 rolled around, the program was on forty-six U.S. stations and thousands of cable outlets in the U.S. and overseas. At the same time we were third in the Neilsen ratings for the time slots when aired. Yet the cost of air time had risen so high that Mama and Dad were using personal funds to help pay the bills.

Mama and Dad finally made the decision to stop production. "It's counter productive," Dad said, "to have to use so much air time asking for money instead of telling viewers about Christ." Besides, they could no longer afford to drain personal funds to finance the show.

God opened a new door for Dad. The Board of Regents of Luther Rice Seminary, an interdenominational school with strong Baptist roots, extended an invitation for him to succeed the much-beloved Dr. Robert Witty, who was retiring as president.

Dad had long admired this world-renowned seminary for its pioneering programs in on-the-field theological education. A number of its graduates were already serving as pastors of some of the largest churches in America.

I moved to Jacksonville, Florida, where the seminary was located before Mama and Dad did. Tim went with me to begin his senior year of high school. Mama and Dad would be coming at the end of the year.

Throughout my life, I often heard the whispering criticisms of peers. "Every time your parents move, you go with them. What are you, joined at the hip?"

No, just the contrary, I would secretly muse. I *enjoy living near Mama and Dad. I'm not there because I'm required to be, but because they let go so easily.*

These peers seemed to be fighting for their own independence, but I already had mine. I exhibited it early on.

As unbelievable as it sounds, I have very clear early memories. I remember my first birthday when my daddy took me to the church early Sunday morning. He sat me on the pew Mama and I always camped on. It was beside the back door in case Mama needed to make a quick dash out with me during the service.

It soon became clear why Daddy and I had gone to church so early. We were practicing the big event. Over and over, he would stand at the front of the church and say, "Do we have any birthdays today?" I would get up from the pew, walk down the aisle and put my single penny in the little church shaped bank. My birthday was a big success. Prissy little Sandee, ruffles and all, executed the birthday march.

So it's understandable why my memory is so clear about my exercise of independence when I was two.

My beautiful Mama, with her flowing auburn hair which framed her porcelain and freckled face, was "June-ing" about the house doing annual spring cleaning. Even the windows were open to air out the stale winter odor. The back door was also open, but the screen door was always locked to "fence me in." Of course, I was a tremendous help as "we" were dusting, mopping and washing clothes.

I remember seeing Mama with a basketful of wet clothes standing near the screen door. Just as she was about to slip out, I saw her turn and look at me, to check if I was safely "occupied" with my building blocks. She then dashed to the clothesline, as she had done many times, and replaced the dry clothes with the wet ones.

Upon entering the house she called, "Sandee, where are you?"

I was no longer "occupied." I was not where I was supposed to be.

She put the basket of dry clothes down and began to look through the house for her little blonde gift from God.

I could hear her search from room to room, looking under the beds, behind the furniture and in the closets. Constantly, she was saying, "Sandee, where are you? Come to Mama." Her voice became more and more panicked.

After looking in every room of the house, she ran out the screen door and began to search the yard. Her voice got louder and louder as she called for her baby. "Sandee, come here, sweetie. Mama can't find you." Mama later told me that she tried to remain calm as she looked behind all the bushes, and finally, on her hands and knees, began to look under the house. Tears were streaming down her face, for I was nowhere to be found.

Grass strains on her dress and hair disheveled, my frightened Mama slowly walked back into the house. She stood in the middle of the kitchen and raised her voice. This time she gave me the full name treatment, which always included my name as well as Dad's. "Sandra Jeanne Miller Williams, I want you out here right this very minute."

Mama stood in silence as she saw a tiny little finger underneath the cloth skirt of the old Sears wringer washing machine. The little finger began to raise up the skirt and a little face peeked out from below. There I was, safe and sound. Mama grabbed me up and proceeded to slobber all over me with tears and kisses. She didn't yell at me, but instead, she affirmed my independence with guidance. "Honey, Mama thought somebody had gotten you. I don't mind you being under the washing machine, but you need to tell Mama when you go off somewhere."

It was obvious that Mama was not afraid of my independence, but she wanted to teach healthy parameters for it. Actually, what Mama taught was "undependence." She was artful at uncoupling, so as an adult I also moved to Lynchburg and Dallas and Jacksonville without the threat of losing myself.

In addition to teaching "undependence," Mama also encouraged us to have a dream in life. "It's always good to have a dream of something you would like to do, or like to see, or like to accomplish. There is nothing in this world that you cannot do. It may take you longer than anyone else to accomplish it, or you might have to learn how to do it, but anything you want to do, you can do."

That encouragement alone propelled me not only to survive Mrs. Grouch but to accomplish many other things. For many years, I was a concert artist in the local church. I have taught in college and graduate schools. I have finished three master's degrees and one-and-a-half doctor's degrees. But my favorite accomplished dream was to have a private counseling practice. Mama and I laughed many times as she said, "Wouldn't Mrs. Grouch have a cow if she could see her 'retarded' student now?"

So my moving to Jacksonville was no big deal. The condition of the seminary's physical plant when Dad stepped into the presidency was another matter. Mama took one look at the cluster of old buildings and knew something had to be done for the students. Since most study was external, the largest gathering of students was graduation week, which became Mama's focus. Her goal was to give them a top notch experience and a pleasant memory to carry back to their pastoral fields.

For the Graduates' Banquet, Mama oversaw planning the menu, table set-up and color coordination. She stayed in the background, with the staff responding cooperatively to her suggestions and requests. They all worked very hard to make this a festive time.

Mama added a President's Reception beforehand, where simple *hors d'oeuvres* were served. Along with the faculty, she and Dad met and greeted graduates and their wives. Then, at Dad's request, each professor hosted a table for the banquet. That gave graduates the opportunity to sit with their major professor.

At Christmastime, Mama and the vice-presidents' wives coordinated a dinner. Mama made a personal call to each faculty/staff wife after the event was planned to tell them when, where and what. This also gave her a chance to express thanks for that person's contribution to the dinner and the seminary.

Mama's spend-ten-dollars-and-look-like-a-million principle carried over to decorating, too. As people commented on the beautification and smoothness of the events, the vice-presidents proudly said, "Miss Dottie did it." Soon, the most frequent comment at seminary special occasions was, "Well, I see Miss Dottie's been in on this."

"To a great degree," Mama often said, "a church takes on the personality of the pastor; a home takes on the personality of the wife; and a seminary takes on the personality of its president." She served to keep the background uncluttered so Dad's personality and ability could shine through.

It never crossed Mama's mind through the past years that this little red-headed girl, straight out of the oil fields of Texas, would be the wife of a seminary president. Mama also told me that the words kept ringing in her head, words that she had tearfully uttered when Dad was called to evangelism: "Here we struggled to get Gene this Doctor of Theology degree. If there's anything an evangelist doesn't need, it's a Doctor of Theology degree. Why did we do that?" She now knew why.

Long before Dad became a seminary president, Mama made birthdays big occasions. She always made the celebrant feel like king or queen for the day. So when Dad's fifty-third birthday drew near, Mama invited Mammaw Miller over for a full day of festivities. After going out for lunch, Mama brought Mammaw by to see me. We visited, then I showed her through my home. It seemed Mammaw was in a pretty good mood, so maybe the evening would be pleasant.

"Well, Iola," Mama turned to Mammaw, "we'd better go get

ready for Gene's big evening out. Do I need to help you with your hair?"

I watched as Mama helped Mammaw into the car, then drove away. Shaking my head, I thought about how Mammaw's actions revealed her selfish philosophy. It was almost like she said, "When you're at my house, I'm the hostess and you do what I want to do. When I'm at your house, I'm the guest and you do what I want to do."

I headed for the bedroom to dress. Before I could take five steps, I heard someone banging at my front door. Hurrying from the back of the house, I spotted Mama's car in my driveway.

"What in the world is wrong?" I asked as Mama frowned and stepped inside, followed by Mammaw. Whatever they were discussing had them both upset. *What is going on?* I wondered.

"Iola," Mama declared, as though I were not there. "I will not put up with your being ugly today. Gene's birthday is not going to be messed up."

Mammaw lit into Mama, screaming, "Don't think for one minute you can talk to me like that. I never did want Gene to marry you. Just a girl out of the oil fields, oil field trash, that's all you were. And he is my son."

"Mammaw, sit down." I led my grandmother to the couch and pulled my chair up in front of her. Up to this point, Mammaw had always gotten my mama off by herself before acting ugly. She wanted to control my dad and anyone who stood in the way, including my mama, was the enemy. "What are you upset about?"

"She's upset with me," Mama stood by the fireplace, hands waving as she spoke. "But I have no idea why."

"I know," Mammaw smugly expressed, as if she had some big secret.

"You know what?" I was trying to sort out my own confusion as to what we were discussing. "What is it that you know?"

"I know the truth."

"What are we talking about?" I asked, still hoping to be a peacemaker. "What truth?"

"Well, I know the truth about Randy."

"You what?" I said. Mama looked like she was absolutely flabbergasted. I stared hard at Dad's mother. "Mammaw, what are you talking about?"

My perplexed Mama said, "Yes, I really would like to know." But Mammaw only focused her eyes on me. "I know that your father is not his father."

"What?"

"That's right. Randy is a bastard."

"Whoa! That is absolutely not true!" I challenged. Mammaw Miller had crossed a boundary and she knew it by the expression on my face. I knew my father and my mama.

My mind flashed back to a summer vacation when Randy was about four years old. Dad drove the car and Mama sat in front beside him. I was mad at Randy, because he wanted to look out the window, instead of playing with me. "Randy," I meanly whispered, so our parents could not hear, "I guess you know you are adopted."

"No, I'm not." Bright little guy that he was, Randy knew what adopted meant.

"Yes, you are," I shot back.

He was quiet for a few minutes, studying the situation. Then he leaned up close to the back of Mama's seat and asked with great projection, "Mama?"

"Yes, darlin'."

"Am I adopted?"

Oh, no! I thought, *I'm in trouble now.*

"Well, Randy," Mama frowned and gave him her undivided attention. "Why would you think something like that?"

"Sandee says I am."

Now Sandra had Mama's undivided attention. "Sandra!" Mama's expression registered acute displeasure.

Mama turned back to Randy and looked him square in the eyes, "Honey, I can promise you, you're not adopted. Mama and Daddy planned to have you. Everybody in the family knew we were asking God for you. You were not even a surprise. We wanted you from the very beginning. On purpose, we had you." So it was impossible to imagine where Mammaw Miller had come up with this outrageous idea.

"Where did you come up with this?" I struggled to remain calm.

"I just know," Mammaw Miller emphatically said.

"How do you know?" I jumped back at her. But she never could give me an explanation, because there was no explanation for this distortion of truth.

Suddenly it all made sense. All the times she had mistreated and slighted Randy, the explanation was right here. Randy's big sister was furious. Even though Randy and I were adults, I felt this big sister urge to fight in his behalf.

"That is an ugly lie, Mammaw. I cannot believe you would think such a horrible thing. You know Mama and Dad have always laughed about Randy being their only planned child and Tim and me being unexpected blessings. You are unable, even at this moment, to back up this accusation with any solid facts. This I must say, is the cruelest, meanest thing you have ever done."

With that, Mammaw pulled out a wad of money and began to hand me twenty-dollar bills. "Mammaw, I don't want your money." But she continued pressing twenty-dollar bills to me.

"Mammaw, I will not be bought off. Do you realize how absolutely horrible you have been to your grandson? Yes, he is your grandson, and you have treated him coldheartedly." With that the money stopped flowing.

Mama had remained by the fireplace, saying nothing. Her eyes were fixed on Mammaw's face and she looked as if she had been hit by a left hook. A few moments later, Mama closed her eyes and took a long deep breath. Finally she spoke. "Iola, we'd better go get dressed. After all, we still have Gene's birthday dinner ahead. None of this will be discussed tonight. Gene will have a happy birthday."

Mammaw looked from one of us to the other, then silently made her way out to the car. Just then, I remembered the money. There were ten twenty-dollar bills in my hand. "Mama, what shall I do with all this money?"

"Honey, keep it. You've earned every dime of it." Mama's voice smiled as I hugged her. "Sandee, I finally know why she has been so ugly to me all these years."

Dad's birthday celebration went off without a hitch. Days later Mama told Dad about our afternoon. After that, we learned that Mammaw had spread her ugly lie throughout the family. Thankfully few, if any, believed her.

But the "family secret" was out.

Mama and I made a special point to give Randy a blow by blow report. While he hadn't known why Mammaw Miller had rejected him, he had come to grips with the situation a long time before. Again, Randy's personality had allowed him to overlook her maliciousness.

Mama was most concerned that Randy know beyond a shadow of a doubt that he was a Williams, through and through. He assured her that he had no doubt of his heritage.

I later asked Mama if she helped Mammaw Miller with her hair that night. "Of course," Mama said, "she's your daddy's mother. I may not like her behavior, but I am commanded by God to honor her."

This was a question of integrity for Mama. Whether Mammaw Miller showed integrity or not, Mama was bound in her commitment to God and to her husband to show respect to someone who had been so cruel to her.

Chapter Twelve

Mama's Special Blessings and Trials

AS TEENAGERS WENT, TIM WAS NEVER DIFFICULT to have around. During his senior year at Terry Parker High School in Jacksonville, Florida, he developed a daily quiet time for devotions, and led several of his friends to the Lord. Sometimes I chuckled to myself as I heard Tim talking with other high schoolers. Of course, looking like a Texan in his boots and hat, his friends called him Tex.

"My dad's in the Mafia."

"Really, Tex?" The kid's eyes got big. "Wow!"

"Yeah, my dad's a hit man." Tim's laugh broke through. "He's in the Mafia for Jesus."

One day, I asked Tim what kept him away from drugs and sex.

"There are three reasons," he explained. "First, I'm scared of God. Then, I'm scared of Dad. Third, I love Mama and don't want to hurt her. Besides, Mama told me that if I ever got arrested, she wouldn't bail me out of jail."

Active in football, baseball, and track, Tim had many friends who worked at McDonald's. Mama always enjoyed the times she took him for an after-school snack at the drive-through. There was one date with Mama that Tim never forgot.

The drive-through speaker was encased in a Ronald McDonald figure. After a few minutes of silence, with no one asking for her order, Mama sang out, "Ronald? Ronald McDonald?" Tim began to slide down on the seat as Mama continued, "Ronald. Where are you, Ronald?"

"Mom!" Tim's face was red, but he couldn't help laughing. "I know these people. Don't do that to me."

Finally, "May I take your order?" sounded from the speaker.

After completing their order, Mama's giggle joined Tim's. Not long after that, she saw Tim coming through the kitchen early in the week. A big smile ringed his face. "Mama, I've got a date Friday night with the cutest cheerleader. She's the cutest thing ever, Mama."

"Well, that's great, Tim." Life went on as usual.

On Thursday, Mama said, "Tim, where are you taking the cheerleader tomorrow night?"

"Oh, I'm not going."

"I thought you had a date. What happened?"

"Well, Mama, it was like this. She came up to me at school, and asked what color underwear I liked. And, Mama, I just didn't feel like I wanted to know what color underwear she was wearing. So I canceled the date."

"I'm so proud of you," Mama said, rejoicing that teaching Tim to make decisions for himself had paid off. "I'm so glad you had the guts to say no, and get out of a situation you were not ready for. You handled that very well," Mama said, as she breathed a prayer of thanks to God.

Tim's goal was to play for the Dallas Cowboys and make a lot of money. One thing was sure, with two preachers in the family already, Tim knew God would not call him as the third one. So he concentrated on sports. When scholarship offers started coming in, he saw education as a tool to get to the pros.

The spring of his graduation, after he planned to play football at Liberty University, Tim and I went to a Christian concert. "I think," Tim said, "as we drove home, that God may be calling me to ministry."

"What kind of ministry?"

"I don't know."

It was clear that something in the concert had spoken to Tim and caused him to question his direction. Searching for answers, Tim decided to go on the road with Dad.

For some reason, Tim had x-rays taken about this time.

When they revealed a stress fracture in his neck, it seemed like a confirmation that he was headed in the right direction. Playing football could easily have led to injury and paralysis.

After nearly two years of travel with Dad, Tim had seen countless people find Jesus. Still he searched for answers. Mama told me later of their conversation.

Tim sat with Mama on the balcony of their beach condo in Jacksonville. "I don't want to preach because my daddy and my brother are preachers. But I don't want not to preach because of that, either. I want to do what God wants."

"Tim, that's a marvelous attitude to have. You're in a good position to hear what the Lord wants you to do. If God calls you to preach, then preach. Your dad and I will be pleased whether you are a preacher or a mechanic or an executive with IBM, as long as it's what God asks of you."

After much soul-searching, Tim announced his call to the ministry, still with no idea how God would use him. Likewise, he had no idea what the anointing of God would mean in that ministry. But, the years have shown that Tim's anointing allows him to reach into the hearts of the lost and draw them to Christ. So, now, it makes perfect sense that he is in full-time evangelism.

"Oh, my," Mama said so many times through the years. "What if I had never accepted this son— this special delivery God sent to us—and missed the joy of Tim? Just think, when I first found out about Tim's existence, I was upset because I selfishly didn't want to go through the baby thing again. I am thankful that God was wiser than I ever could be.

"Now if He would just show me how to deal with your grandmother."

And Mama needed every bit of wisdom the Lord would grant her when it came to dealing with Dad's troublesome mother. While we were living in Dallas, Mammaw Miller was living near her sister, Gladys, in Corsicana, Texas. Mama and Dad both tried to be patient with her and respectful to her. But at times it was difficult

During that time it was not unusual for Dad to fly into the airport and make a run to see his mother. So it was, upon his return from an overseas meeting that Dad dropped Mama off at the house and headed across town

Mama was talking to a friend on the phone later when Dad drove in from seeing his mother. She was still on the phone when she heard Dad come in and walk up the stairs. "Oh, my," Mama told her telephone pal, "something must be wrong. He's barely had time to get there and back, let alone have a visit."

Hanging up the phone, Mama followed Dad upstairs. She heard Dad in their room, crying as though his heart were broken. *Is his mother dead*? she wondered. Mama sat beside Dad on the bed. "What on earth has happened, Gene?"

Through his tears, Dad managed to say, "My . . . my mother doesn't love me."

"What do you mean 'doesn't love me'?"

"Well, I went to visit her. Instead of welcoming me, she hollered and screamed, 'I don't love you'."

"Well," Mama drew in a big breath. "We both know that's not true. If anything, she's loved you too much. She wanted to control you and your life."

"But why did she say something like this to me?"

Searching for the right words, Mama said, "First of all, I can't help but believe your mother does love you. Let's not fool ourselves, she loves herself more. But Iola's love is a selfish love, no matter who it's with. There's no doubt in my mind that your mother loves you. In her own way, of course. The saddest thing about this is that you never had the kind of mother's love you deserved."

Mama told me about their conversation and I relayed the story to Aunt Fran, Mammaw's other sister. "I'm not sure anyone has ever realized this," Aunt Fran said, "but my sister is sick."

I'd been struggling with this myself. It was Aunt Fran's pronouncement that pushed me into accepting reality. Dad's mother, my grandmother, was a classic borderline personality with extensive psychological complications. Oftentimes it is difficult to accept that a member of your own family has a mental health problem. But, by accepting this, I better understood her behavioral history and the anger toward her that had festered in my mind for so long began to find peace.

After that, I watched Mama and Dad be very kind and gracious to Mammaw. When they moved to Jacksonville they moved her to a seniors' residence nearby. They visited her, no matter how mean and unkind she was. Weekly, Mama washed her clothes and managed to do her hair and nails. Mama was indeed teaching Dad how to love.

It nearly broke my heart when Dad told of one visit. He had held Mammaw's hand after she had lost her speech. He told us later of wondering, *What ugly things would she be saying to me if she could talk?*

Mama never questioned Dad's love for his mother. Neither did she question the love that was the cornerstone of their marriage. Dad had kept his commitment to love and protect Mama always, even if it was to protect her from his own mother.

Knowing Mammaw's cruelty never changed the respect and honor Mama and Dad showed her as long as she lived. Over and over, Mama showed Dad that real love, the love his mother was never able to give him, did not mean having to control the other person. Instead, it set the person free to be all that God wanted and expected.

Finally, death came to Mammaw about two o'clock in the afternoon of July 5, 1984. Mama and Dad were at the beach condo celebrating their wedding anniversary. After learning of Mammaw Miller's death Dad said, "Now, Dottie, I know you think my mother did this on purpose."

"Yes, I do," she quickly responded with a little smile. "You'll never convince me otherwise. She died on our wedding anniversary on purpose. Just to mess it up."

Iola Miller had outlived most of her generation. A few people, her sisters and some of their friends, came to the funeral. The service was cold, with not a tear shed.

When it was almost time to go to the gravesite, I stood beside Dad. He looked into the casket at his mother's face for the last time. All at once, tears streaked down his cheeks.

"Mama," I moved to where she stood. "Dad's crying."

"He's crying?" She looked at me like, *You've got to be kid-*

ding. "He's crying?"

"Yes."

I watched Mama walk up beside Dad and take his hand in hers. Within a minute, his tears stopped. Later, when Mama and Dad talked, he explained, "I was crying because I never had a real mother."

"You know," Randy summed it up for us later, "the saddest thing about this funeral was that it wasn't sadder."

After the funeral, Mama and I went to a park and sat on a picnic table to talk. "Mama, do you remember times during the last thirty years when I did something family members did not like? No matter whether it was right or wrong, they always called me Iola. It was kind of like everybody's idea of saying, 'I disapprove of you right now'."

"Yes, honey, I do."

"I know, now, that they were trying to show me that I should not behave like she did. But back then, I thought they were saying, 'You are Mammaw Miller.' It was an insult, and it hurt. I knew how everybody felt about her, and I concluded they thought the same about me."

"Honey, I had no idea you had that impression."

"Well, it took me thirty years to figure it out. But, Mama, I am not her. I cannot and will not be cruel and mean like she was. It's been almost like the family expected me to pick up her baton and take her place. I simply refuse to do that."

"Honey, it never crossed my mind that you would take her place."

Mama's wisdom, over the years, had played out ways of handling difficult situations before me. We talked about my interest in helping others through counseling. Now, Mama encouraged me to do the work I felt God calling me to.

The generation in which I grew up did not accept a Christian's need for counseling. The common thought was that only people who had something wrong with their Christianity or spiritual growth—people lost or fallen from the Lord—sought counseling. Christians buried their heads in the sand about sexual abuse, incest, spousal abuse, and any kind of dysfunction. In the process, we just created more of it. My questions became like sandpaper, rubbing against the pat answers. "I don't know why people would go to a counselor," Dad said at the beginning. "We never had to go to one."

"We probably should have," I remember Mama saying, "because of your mother. Back when we were dealing with her, we probably should have gotten help to know how to deal with her better. Gene, don't mistake Sandee's doing this type of work as something anti-God."

Knowing Mama understood counseling's positive potential, I challenged my dad. "If you, the preachers, do not talk about things like sexual abuse from the pulpit, it will continue. We gladly talk about dancing, drinking, and smoking, but we've denied the existence of a generation of sexually abused children. The ones now in abusive situations are denied permission to come to the church to talk about and deal with it.

"I think it's wonderful that an alcoholic can get saved and be miraculously rescued from alcohol. But, what about the man who struggles with alcohol every single day? Do we question his salvation, just because it's a struggle for him?

"The fact is, God deals with the recovery from alcohol in everyone individually. He deals with everyone exactly where their hearts and needs are. There's no formula for this. Except that Jesus Christ is the power source for the Christian that the lost man does not have."

By the time I set up practice, counselors had come to the jumping off point, where we were usable in the Christian community.

"Sandee," Mama reminded me, "Iola has given you tools for discernment and understanding that many counselors don't have. God can make positive use of your grandmother's negative behavior through all the insight you've gained by watching her."

Mama's words have proven true many times over. Because of Mammaw Miller, I am able to see dysfunction. My goal as counselor is always to bring the person or family to the point where they will let God work in their lives.

No matter what my mama was faced with, she always knew

that God could use it for good. We often talked about Romans 8:28, which says, "And we know that all things work together for good to them that love God, to them who are called according to *His* purpose."

"Sandee," she reminded, "that Scripture doesn't say that all things that happen to Christians are good. Or that they feel good. Or that they turn out to be good. Romans 8:28 is saying that all things can work together for good. And the goodness that can result is seen in the beginning of the next verse. 'For whom He did foreknow, He also did predestinate *to be* conformed to the image of his Son . . .'."

I sat by Mama and her open Bible, nodding my understanding. Mama was teaching me what the desire of every Christian should be: to become more like Jesus, no matter what our life situation might be. Whether we were dealing with special blessings or special trials.

Not only did she teach us this principle from the Word, but by her example as well.

Chapter Thirteen

Mama's Little Difficulties

THE ASIAN FLU HIT THE COUNTRY SEVERELY back in 1978. Bless Mama's heart, she got it three times in a row. The last episode was the worst. When it seemed she was unable to shake the virus, Dr. Guthrie, her family physician at the time, ordered some tests. One test came back with a bright red flag. It seemed that the virus had attacked Mama's pancreas, and she was now a brittle, adolescent-type diabetic.

We heard "diabetes" but Mama heard the word "opportunity." She learned to shoot herself with insulin and follow a diabetic diet. She soon brought her condition under control.

Her endocrinologist in 1985 was Dr. Montgomery at the Joslin Diabetic Center in Jacksonville. Dr. Montgomery was most concerned because Mama had a cold that only seemed to get worse. Mama was pretty good about taking her medicines, so it was no problem to add an antibiotic to the list, even though she was in the throes of Tim's wedding preparation. Mama knew the importance of a son's wedding because of the lovely ceremony Randy and his Georgia bride, Christa, had in Atlanta in December of 1976. Now it was Tim who was marrying Joy, daughter of Dr. and Mrs. Jerry Vines. He was co-pastor with Dr. Homer Lindsay of the First Baptist Church of Jacksonville.

A few days before the wedding festivities, I ran over to Mama's to see how she was doing. Her skin was gray and she was complaining of a pain around her ribcage. We called Dad to come home from the seminary so we could get Mama to the doctor. Dr. Montgomery took one look at her and said, "You are going into the hospital, and I'm not arguing about it. You have pneumonia, and if I don't get you on some IV antibiotics, you are going to die."

"But . . . but, my son, Tim's wedding is Saturday. I just can't be sick," Mama pleaded.

"Wedding or no wedding, I can't help that. You're going into the hospital right now," ordered Dr. Montgomery.

"Well, can I go get some lunch? I haven't had anything to eat."

"No, we'll get you some in the hospital."

"You promise? Are you sure?"

"I'm putting you on a special diabetic wing. Since it's noon, I'm writing orders right now to make sure you get food immediately."

Mama was not a happy camper, but she complied until the dinner trays were brought and there was no tray for her. Mama spoke to the nurse, "I have not eaten since early this morning. I am a diabetic and I must have some food. Dr. Montgomery ordered food for me."

The time moved by slowly and by eight o'clock that night, she still had not heard from the nurse or the dietician. It was like she was a prisoner in the bed because of the IVs. She was unable to fend for herself. Her family was tied up with wedding commitments, unreachable, and did not know she was in trouble.

Mama began to feel very strange, clammy and shaky. She began calling the nurses' station more frequently, begging for food. Nine o'clock rolled around and Mama's nurse finally entered the room. In her hand was a syringe of insulin. "What are you doing?" Mama quizzed.

"I'm going to give you your insulin."

"NO YOU ARE NOT! Let me make something perfectly clear. I have been asking, no begging for food for nine hours. Now you're coming in, trying to give me an insulin shot when I have not eaten. Have you lost your mind? What does a person have to do around here to get a tray of food? I'll tell you what I'll do. I'll just call Channel Twelve and tell them there's a little old lady at this hospital who can't get any food. And, they're trying to kill her by giving her insulin shots."

"Ma'am," the nurse responded. "It's too late to get you a

tray. The best I can do is some Rice Krispies and milk."

"Mercy!" Mama shook her head. "You're telling me that you're a diabetic nurse and you don't know that Rice Krispies is loaded with sugar?"

At that point the phone rang with a heaven-sent call. Mama's friend, Shirley Lindsay, was checking on her. "Dottie, what is the matter? You sound upset."

It didn't take long for Mama to relate the happenings of the day. Shirley said she'd see what she could do. Mama had no idea that "what she could do," was call a board member of the hospital. Within thirty minutes, my mama was eating a hot tray of food. "Just another of life's little inconveniences," Mama would say.

As for the wedding, Mama sweet-talked Dr. Montgomery into letting her check out of the hospital for a few hours. Her wrist corsage covered the disconnected IV needles. She looked like death warmed over, but she wouldn't have missed seeing her youngest child's wedding for anything in the world. After all, she always knew he was a special delivery package.

Mama survived that hospital adventure, and had no noticeable health problems for almost two years. In January of 1987, Dad took off with several pastors for an evangelistic crusade in Nigeria. Mama and I planned to take some of the wives and meet them in London, England.

"Something's happening to me," Mama said, as I drove us to the Jacksonville airport. "And I don't know what it is."

"What do you mean?" I held the wheel tight, knowing Mama did not complain without reason.

"Something's wrong with the left side of my face. It feels strange and it doesn't move."

Memories of her experience in Texas came rushing back. Fear gripped me as I pulled the car up to the curb. *I hope it's not another stroke*.

"Oh, Mama." Her left eye did not blink with the right one, and saliva trickled from the left side of her mouth. "Mama, I don't want to alarm you, but your face looks like it did after Tim was born. We'd better go back home and call your doctor."

"No, Sandee, your dad will be worried if we don't show up." Mama flexed her left leg and arm. "This can't be too serious. Nothing but my face is affected, so we're going to go on."

I knew that determined look, and go we did. Thankfully no new symptoms developed enroute. Once in London, we had about forty-eight hours before Dad's arrival. Mama, knowing she must have an answer for Dad, agreed to see a doctor.

"You have Bell's Palsy, Mrs. Williams." I felt myself relax a little at the doctor's words. "Most of these cases resolve with time. Just don't over extend yourself."

Back in our room, we laughed as Mama practiced her half-smile in front of the mirror. Finally she said, "Sandra, we have a decision to make. Which side of my face will we keep, and which side will we throw away?"

By the time Dad came in, she teased, "Well, honey, the old girl ain't what she used to be."

Back home, Mama had one big concern. She had made a commitment to speak at a conference with several hundred pastor's wives in attendance. Although Mama's slurred speech was better, her left eye still watered. She was concerned that she wouldn't be able to see her notes or control the drool. "Well," she decided, "it seems that the same God who allowed this paralysis knew I was scheduled to speak. Unless He tells me otherwise, I'd better be there."

Again, another of life's little difficulties allowed Mama the opportunity to show courage and self-sacrifice. No further evidence of health problems became obvious for almost two years.

The family headed for Las Vegas and the Southern Baptist Convention in June of 1989. I stayed behind to see counseling clients. On the afternoon of the day the convention opened, I dialed the Hilton, and asked for Mama and Dad's room.

Mama answered the phone with a cough and her voice sounded a little tired. "I'm the only one here," she said. I'm resting up before your dad takes us all out to eat tonight."

"Is it hard to find seats for the meetings?"

"It's crowded. Today, we kept our seats over lunch. Christa and I walked to a sub shop and brought back sandwiches and cold drinks for the family."

"That sounds good."

"Oh, they were delicious. Now I'm just tired and thirsty. I've already had two Cokes since I came to the room, but . . . "

Mama coughed several times.

"Are you all right, Mama?"

Mama's voice sounded strained. "Honey, I'm going to have to hang up." Cough, cough. "Stuff is coming up out of my throat, and I can't stop coughing."

Click.

I waited ten minutes, then redialed the hotel. Her line was busy. At this point, I didn't know enough to be worried. Later, as we pieced the events together, I understood why I should have been.

After hanging up, Mama sat on the side of the bed. Her explosive coughs sent phlegm flying across the room. Between coughs, something gurgled inside her chest. Her choppy breathing got harder and faster. Still unsure what was happening, Mama had the sense to pick up the phone and dial 0.

"Operator" came the voice from the front desk.

"This is Mrs. Williams." Mama cleared her throat. "I've become ill very quickly and I'm going to need some help." Another spasm interrupted. "I'll unlock my door and leave it ajar. You send help."

"They'll be right there. Don't hang up."

Mama crossed the room and opened her door. Coughing spasms continued as she dragged herself back to the bed and sat down. Just then, two security men arrived.

"Mrs. Williams?" The first one went to Mama's side. "We're here to help."

"Mrs. Williams," the other one asked as he picked up the phone, "is there anyone else of your party in the hotel now?"

"No, my family's all at the convention hall. My husband, Gene Williams, and our sons, Tim and Randy."

He relayed that information to the operator, who then called the convention hall to have Dad and my brothers paged.

Within minutes, two EMTs carrying a stretcher burst through

Mama's door. One slapped a stethoscope to Mama's chest. "Have you ever had congestive heart failure?" he asked.

"No, but my mother did."

The second EMT radioed the hospital for orders. Mama's IV and heart monitor were soon in place. Oxygen flowed through green plastic tubing which ended as prongs in Mama's nostrils. Orders came to start Lasix through the IV.

"Mrs. Williams," the security guard asked, "do you know anyone else who is in the hotel now?"

"Lea Stanley came in when I did." The EMTs had Mama on their stretcher, with her head propped up. Frequent coughs punctuated her speech. "Her room is just down the hall."

Someone went for Lea, and brought her into Mama's room.

The security man relayed a message from the operator, "No one is answering the page at the convention hall."

"Dottie," Lea offered, trying to stay calm. "Have they tried the phone in the Luther Rice Seminary booth?"

"Please try it, Lea." Mama kept coughing. The EMTs began wheeling her toward the door, as she called, "Please, find Gene."

Lea began dialing. "Don't worry, Dottie. I'll find him." And that she did. Shortly, Dad was on his way to the hospital.

Sirens and lights going, the ambulance whisked Mama across town. As she saw the gambling hotels rapidly passing, Mama prayed. *God, please don't let me die in Las Vegas. How will my kids ever explain it?*

Phone calls kept me updated through the next several days as I struggled to stay put in Jacksonville. However, if I had known what lay ahead, I would have flown out on the next plane.

After forty-eight hours in the CCU, Mama's doctors decided, "We're going to remove your IV and step you down to a regular semi-private room."

Finally, a nurse maneuvered Mama's wheelchair down the hall toward the last available bed. "Someone," Mama said, as they neared her room's door, "is coughing her head off."

That terrible cough sounded again. This time, Mama realized it came from the other half of her new room. The nurse caring for Mama's new roommate stepped away from the other bed, removed her mask, and washed her hands. Before leaving the room, the nurse washed her hands again. *Uh oh,* Mama wondered, *What in the world is wrong with this woman in my room?*

After a few minutes, the coughing woman grew quiet.

"I believe," Mama fished for an explanation, "your cough is even worse than the one I had when I came in with congested heart failure."

"Yes, it's really bad." The roommate confirmed Mama's worst thought, "They tell me I have TB."

"Oh, great," Mama mumbled under her breath, as she hotfooted it to the nurses station, heart monitors and all. "My roommate just told me she has TB. Is that correct?"

"Mrs. Williams," the desk nurse replied, "we are not allowed to discuss the other patients with you."

"Then, please find me another room. She is infectious, or you wouldn't be wearing masks to take care of her."

"I'm sorry, Mrs. Williams, but there is no other bed open in the entire hospital."

Mama didn't argue with them anymore. Still, she didn't know what to do. *One thing is for certain,* Mama thought, *I may be assigned that room, but I'm not sleeping in that room. All I need is TB. Lord, help me*. Gathering up her pillows and blanket, Mama, trying to look casual, trucked down the hall with heart monitor still in tow. Calling a cab and going back to the hotel sounded like the best idea, but it wasn't practical for now. Just then Mama found a sunroom-waiting area with a couch. She settled there and fell asleep.

A touch on the shoulder awakened her. "Mrs. Williams?" A panicked nurse stood at her side. "What are you doing out here? We have looked all over the hospital for you."

Mama calmly but emphatically stated, "I have enough health problems without being in a room with someone contagious. I will not stay in that room. If you don't have another bed to put me in, then this is my room."

And that's where she stayed.

Mama's Las Vegas doctors insisted on a cardiac catheterization. "We must assess any heart damage before we can let you go home." Mama hesitantly agreed.

"I'll tell you, fellows," Mama joked with the young doctors, on the big morning, "this had better be good. They're not going to let me go back to Florida if you don't find the right thing. And, I want to go home."

All eyes were on the TV screen as the doctor threaded the long catheter toward Mama's heart. All at once, one of the young men burst out singing. "I'm Going Back to Jacksonville." Mama laughed with the rest.

"No," Mama asserted, when her doctors wanted to extend her stay a few more days. "I will not stay here another minute. I will go to the hotel and wear your monitor. When twenty-four hours is up, I'll get in the cab and come back out here. But, I will not stay in that room with a TB patient."

Mama had struck a deal. When read, the test results showed very little damage to her heart. She was homeward bound and searching for a cardiologist.

There still was no real answer to why Mama had this episode. She always believed that she overloaded on salt. The amount she took in might not have been too much for anyone else, but it was for her.

My mama was an amazing woman. When she experienced life's problems and difficulties, she would say, "That's just one of life's 'little' inconveniences." While facing these little inconveniences, she saw herself like a kid jumping the waves at the beach. When the big waves knock you down, you just get right back up and keep on jumping. Sometimes I thought my mama was unsinkable. Until my birthday, that is.

I was sleeping late. After all, it was my birthday—February 16, 1990. The phone, absolutely ringing off the wall, forced me to struggle out of a deep sleep. It was barely light outside as I grabbed the receiver, wondering who would call me at this hour. Everyone I knew was aware that I always took the day off on my birthday. *Surely my baby brothers aren't calling this early in the morning,*

Placing the phone to my ear, I cleared my throat and finally got out, "Hello."

"Sandra," I heard on the other end. I recognized that voice, and knew that when my mama used "Sandra," I needed to really pay attention.

"Yes?"

"Sandra, are you awake?"

"Yes." Of course, I was halfway telling the truth, because I was only halfway awake.

"Honey, I'm going to need your help today. I'm not feeling very well." Then Mama's sobs began to break through. "I don't understand what's happening to me. Every time I turn around, I start feeling bad. I just don't understand this."

Fully awake by now and concerned, I asked, "Mama, what time would you like for me to be there?"

"You better get here early. There's an awful lot to do."

"Let me get dressed," I said, "and I . . . I'll be there as soon as possible."

"Okay, honey. I'm so sorry to have to inconvenience you on your birthday."

Amazing, I thought. *Inconvenience me on my birthday? How like Mama to forget how difficult it was and how "inconvenient" to have brought me into this world*. It didn't matter what day it was, Mama needed help and I was going. Saying "no" never even crossed my mind. "Mama, that's fine. I'll be there as soon as I can get there. Okay? Bye-bye." We both hung up the phone.

As I worried about the panic in Mama's voice, I figured it was because today was a very important day. Besides celebrating my birthday, Mama was to speak to the pastors' wives at the First Baptist Church of Jacksonville's Pastors' Conference She had worked hard at preparing her presentation and was so excited to have been invited. Wasting no time, I dressed and drove across town.

When I arrived, I found Mama sitting in a chair, working at every breath she took. She had already taken some extra Lasix, hoping that would clear up any fluid collected in her lungs.

"Mama," I tried, after looking at her, "don't you think, maybe, we should cancel your speaking today?"

With a half smile, Mama looked at me and said, "Oh, honey,

I can't do that. I just need a little help and I'll be all right. I'll be able to make it." Obviously, the only thing that would keep my determined Mama from speaking to these ladies would be an appointment at the Pearly Gates.

Mama ate the light breakfast I prepared. Then, with her seated before me, I began applying her makeup. As we finished, Mama decided she needed to rest a while. I helped her to the chair in front of the television and she tuned in her regular channel, QVC.

Although my mama could no longer go to Bargain Gusher in Houston, she considered QVC a good substitute, at times. After all, once a Bargain Gusher shopper, always a Bargain Gusher shopper. As she rested, her breathing grew easier.

"Honey, I'm feeling better," Mama said, after about an hour. "I think I'm ready for you to fix my hair." In no time, she was ready to go. Loaded in the car, we headed downtown, and arrived just in time for her to speak.

As Mama was being introduced, I saw her reach into her purse. Very discreetly she pulled out a nitroglycerin tablet. Just as the welcoming applause began, Mama popped the tablet under her tongue, stood up and headed for the platform.

Cocking her head, and with a twinkle in her eye, Mama began. "In Proverbs 31, it says, 'Who can find a virtuous woman? For her price is far above rubies.' You know, ladies, a virtuous woman today is sometimes very hard to find. We, as women, need to set ourselves apart and hold respect for ourselves. We need to value and treasure ourselves, and let that determine how we behave. In God's eyes, we are precious, precious gems. And if we live a dedicated life, that gem will become more valuable as the years go by.

"Looking now at verses 11 and 12," Mama continued, "it says, 'The heart of her husband doth safely trust in her, so that he shall have no need of spoil. She will do him good, and not evil, all the days of her life.'

"Trust," Mama said, "is the core of a relationship. Something a couple should protect at all costs. A wife should declare to her husband that everything she does is for his good, and not intended for any evil. Now, what are some ways the woman can do evil in the life of her husband?

"One is with regard to the children," Mama continued. "Never undermine your husband's authority in the home," she told her audience. "Remember that one day your little ones will be teenagers. And those teenagers will be bigger than you are, ladies. And, if for no reason other than sheer physical size, you'll definitely need your husband then. But that's only one reason why you need to maintain your husband's authority in the lives of your children.

"Another reason is that they need to have a healthy attitude toward the authority of their father. It is important that you are cautious to help your children have a good father-child relationship. When the husband's back is turned, the wife should pat him on the back, and not stab him in the back.

"Always remember," Mama told the ladies. She paused briefly, took a sip of water, then continued. "Remember that the long-term costs of anything less will show up in the lives of the children. Remember that children are on temporary loan from God. They are in our care to be raised in honor and glory to the Lord.

"This, of course, brings me to another way a woman can do evil in the home." Mama paused, as though to underline her next words. "Oftentimes in Christian homes, especially in the homes of ministers, wives and husbands will minister to the church with a smiling face. And then, when they go home, they 'act like the devil.' This inconsistency in the lives of the parents is seen in the devastated lives of some preacher's kids."

I was sitting close enough to the platform to see that sweat had broken out on Mama's face. She was no longer using her hands as she always did but instead had grabbed hold of the side of the podium. Fear pierced my heart.

"Ladies, there is another way in which a woman can do evil in her home." Mama struggled as she continued. "Evil will come out of any woman who tries to play God in her home. Any woman who tries to play God in the life of her husband, and does not allow her husband to seek God's direction in the home is inviting trouble." Mama's breathing was becoming more labored as she went on. "Over the years, I've sat at many a table and heard many a preacher's wife say, 'We're not leaving this pastorate. We're not leaving this church 'til these kids graduate from high school.' What God had for this man to do was irrelevant to this pastor's wife, because she was intervening and encroaching on God's territory.

"Oh, ladies," Mama took a deep breath, "we must have a healthy respect and a reverence for God Almighty. It is not our job nor our place to manage the ministries of our husbands."

Mama reached into her pocket and took out several tissues, then began to wipe her face and forehead. "Now, ladies, let's continue through the passage. 'She seeketh wool, and flax, and worketh willingly with her hands. She is like the merchant's ships; she bringeth her food from afar. She riseth also while it is yet night, and giveth food to her household, and a portion to her maidens.' Proverbs 31:13-15.

"The woman in Proverbs was a hard worker," Mama noted. "She labored and sacrificed. She got up before dawn to prepare breakfast for her family. And she was a gracious woman who gave, even to her household help. Now, ladies, let's be honest with ourselves. Being a wife and mother-homemaker can sometimes be a pain in the neck. Nothing is glorious about changing diapers," she said. "And there is no great joy in cleaning toilets either. But we have a choice. We can gripe and complain about the drudgery of those tasks, or we can emulate the woman of Proverbs and do them with delight.

"Now, does 'doing them with delight' make the work any easier?" Mama paused and wiped her face again with a tissue. "Of course not. But it could make it more pleasant for you and your family. Especially when you tackle this work with delight instead of complaint."

It was about this time that Mama reached into the inside pocket of her jacket and pulled out another nitroglycerin tablet. Having popped it into her mouth, she continued, while I prayed, *God, get Mama through this. Don't let her die now.*

Mama went on. "'She considereth a field, and buyeth it; with the fruit of her hands she planteth a vineyard. She girdeth her loins with strength, and strengtheneth her arms. She perceiveth that her merchandise is good; her lamp goeth not out by night. She layeth her hands to the spindle, and her hands hold the distaff.' (Proverbs 31:16-19)

"Now let's look further down to verses 24 and 25," Mama continued. "'She maketh fine linen, and selleth it, and delivereth girdles unto the merchants. Strength and honor are her clothing, and she shall rejoice in time to come.'

"Well," Mama leaned her head back and, to my amazement, giggled. "Now, ladies, this Proverbs woman had a good business head on her shoulders. She invested in a field and planted a vineyard in good soil. To earn money from her harvest, she took the grapes to market. She was no milquetoast gal, she possessed great inner strength. She was a good business woman who planned ahead."

It seemed at that moment, Mama had exhausted nearly all of her strength. She began to breathe more heavily as she moved on through the passage. "'She stretcheth out her hand to the poor; yea, she reacheth forth her hand to the needy.' Proverbs 31:20.

"I think there is no doubt," Mama continued, "that the Proverbs woman was not selfish. Not only did she give to her husband and children, but she also helped those who were less fortunate than she.

"Then, ladies, you'll notice in verses 21 and 22, that the lady of Proverbs was a very sharp dresser. 'She is not afraid of the snow for her household; for all her household are clothed with scarlet. She maketh coverings of tapestry; her clothing is silk purple.'

"Now I can imagine that this gal is very frugal. She probably bought much of her wardrobe from Bargain Gusher. She looked for bargains, but she didn't buy 'cheap' stuff either. Scarlet and purple were the colors of royalty. Everything she purchased was designed to make her husband, her children and herself look good."

At this point, I wasn't sure if Mama was going to make it through the rest of her presentation. She drew one very long breath and hastened toward the conclusion.

"Proverbs 31:23 tells us, 'Her husband is known in the gates, when he sitteth among the elders of the land.' And, looking down at verse 26, 'She openeth her mouth with wisdom, and her tongue is the law of kindness.' And, in verse 30, it says, 'Her children rise up, and call her blessed; her husband also, and he praiseth her, saying, 'Many daughters have done virtuously, but thou excellest them all. Favor is deceitful, and beauty is vain, but a woman who feareth the Lord, she shall be praised.'

"I must say," Mama continued, "that the Proverbs woman didn't do things to embarrass her husband, her family or herself. Above all, she did not do things to embarrass God.

"When her husband sat among the elders, he was known for the character of his wife and children. This woman of Israel didn't put her husband in financial jeopardy. She didn't act so foolish as to put him in social jeopardy either. The husband of our lady of Proverbs could walk through the streets with his head high. Not out of pride, but out of thankfulness for the treasure he had in his wife. A wife who was very wise as to the things that are important."

Mama, being a wise woman herself, knew that she had gone the distance and now she was finished. She slowly walked to the first chair available, as applause filled the auditorium. After a brief rest and without much ado, Mama and I slipped out to head home. *Thank you, Lord,* I breathed. *Oh, thank you for getting Mama through this.*

In the car, I asked Mama, "Do we need to go to the hospital, or go by to see the doctor?

"No," she said. "I think the fullness in my chest is beginning to leave. I'm feeling a little bit better, but I am very, very weary. Let's just go home, so I can rest."

After getting her settled, I hung around the house a while, to see how she would do. Mama quickly fell asleep, and I began to think of the words she had said to the women at the Pastor's Conference. Without a doubt in my mind, my Mama took the woman of Proverbs as her example because she lived out those principles. Mama's husband and children did indeed rise up and call her blessed.

Chapter Fourteen

Mama and Her Grandchildren

MAMA WAS SO PLEASED WHEN REAGAN, her first grandchild, was born to Randy and Christa. Mama called me from the hospital and was just absolutely thrilled that little Reagan could hold his head up, as if none of the other babies could.

About three years later, Reagan became a big brother to Judson. One day, when Judson was three years old, the family was all coming in for dinner after Mama and Dad moved to the Jacksonville Beach condo. Mama's favorite pastry shop made chocolate sheet cake almost as good as Mammaw Fiew's had been, so she ordered one for our dessert.

When Mama arrived at the shop, it was obvious that the help had had a busy day. The sales lady showed Mama the frosted cake. "This cake may be a little over-baked, Mrs. Williams." Mama glanced at her watch and saw there was no time to bake another. Seeing Mama frown, the sales lady added, "Oh, I'm sure it will be all right."

"I certainly hope so," Mama sighed as she paid for the cake.

Mama dutifully brought the cake home and began putting the rest of the meal together. By the time she set the table, everybody had arrived.

Mama got plenty of compliments on her cooking. "I've saved the best for last," she said as she headed for the kitchen to get the cake.

"Oh, no," we heard her moan. All eyes watched Mama set the sorry-looking desert on the table. The cake, dry from overbaking, had soaked up moisture from the frosting, creating an uneven trim.

"Well," Randy quipped. "We always knew Mama couldn't bake a decent cake. Now, it looks like she can't even buy one." Laughter rolled around the table. The only one to eat any of that cake was Judson. He didn't seem to mind its dryness at all.

With each of her grandsons, Mama got a big chuckle because they had the Williams stamp on the back of their necks which was identical to the same strawberry birthmark that their Granddad had on his neck. We all remembered Mammaw Miller's crazy charge that Randy was not Dad's son. "There's certainly no doubt about who their grandfather is," Mama chirped. "Isn't it great that God has a sense of humor?"

Mama and Dad phoned their grandsons almost every Saturday morning. And, as soon as the boys were big enough, they started coming for a week at a time to Grandmother's house.

The highlight of each summer was a trip to Disney World at Orlando. It didn't matter that Mama wasn't feeling well. "I'm not going to let my aches and pains keep Reagan and Judson from having a good time," she vowed. Mama weathered the hottest days of the Florida summer, to see those bright little eyes light on Mickey Mouse.

Tim and Joy's Brittney came next. Joy asked if I would be in the delivery room with her and Tim. Of course, I said yes. So, on a warm June night, as the grandparents sat in the waiting room, I watched that precious little girl enter the world.

Immediately, I felt that I recognized her nose but couldn't place where I had seen it before. As I continued to study Brittney's face, It suddenly clicked. It was as if God had taken Mama's nose and placed it in little bitty form on her first granddaughter.

As Joy completed her work commitment, Mama was blessed with babysitting Brittney one day a week. A special love quickly developed between them kind of like they had been friends for a long, long time.

Mama supported the parenting styles of her children. She didn't spend her energy judging a style's rightness or wrongness but affirmed to her grandchildren that their Mama and Daddy were right. "When you visit Grandmother, we've got to keep the same rules that you have at home," she said. Once in a while, Mama had a special opportunity to have a powerful effect on one of her grandkids. At one of our family reunions before Judson started school, he and Mama had a heart-to-heart talk.

Mama had carried tiny baby Brittney to the bedroom for a nap, while her mother, Joy visited. Mama told us later that five-year-old Judson came to the bedroom door, cracked it, peeked in, and then backed away. Finally, after he did this three or four times, Mama motioned him in. She threw some pillows on the floor so they could talk without waking the baby.

"Grandmother," Judson said, "I don't think I'm going to do as well in school as Reagan."

"Has Mother or Daddy said anything to you about that?"

"No."

"I think that your Mother and Daddy expect you to do what Judson can do. You do Judson's best work, and they'll be very satisfied."

"Well. . ., but, I'm not as smart as Reagan."

"I don't know about that. Now, your big brother is very smart and does very well in school. But, you know, not all the Williamses made straight As."

"Really?"

"I think there have been some C's made, lots of B's, and a few D's. And maybe even an F or two."

Judson's little eyes got big. Up to now, he thought he was the only Williams that might not do well in school.

"Now," Mama continued, as Judson studied her face. "Your daddy is not exactly like Uncle Tim, is he? And Uncle Tim isn't exactly like your daddy. They are both terrific fellows, but they're not just alike. And you don't have to be just like Reagan. God made you and gave you your own personality and gifts. Your gifts may not be like Reagan's, but they are just right for Judson."

With Brittney asleep on the bed, Mama brought Judson out where the family was gathered. "Christa," Mama said to his mother, "did you ever make a B in school?"

"Oh, yes. In fact, I think I made a C."

Without telling us why, Mama asked each of us, including Dad, about our school grades. Then Mama turned to Judson and said, "See, not all the Williamses make straight A's, so you're going to be fine."

With that, Judson's face showed relief. He charged outside for bigger and better things.

"I am so pleased," Mama said, after filling Christa and Randy in on what had prompted the conversation with their son about grades. "You're not making two peas-in-a-pod of your sons. Instead, you are letting each of your children take what God has given him and use it to be the best individual he can be."

Mama was always "Grandmother" and Dad "Granddad" to Reagan and Judson. That was alright for them, but Brittney had her own names in mind for Mama and Dad—"Grandmommie" and "Papa Doc." Mama, always willing to applaud a child's individuality, answered to her new name with a smile.

One summer after Mama began feeling more and more exhausted, Reagan came for his regular visit. With a quizzical look on his face, he approached Mama. "I would like to know what's going on."

"What do you mean?"

"I used to come for two weeks with you, then I started coming for ten days, and now I only get to stay a week. I want to know what's going on."

"Well, it's me that's going on," his grandmother explained. "It's because I'm not really well. I don't really know why, Reagan, but I just don't feel well. I can hold up about a week and that's about it." Knowing Mama's habitual honesty with him, Reagan accepted her answer and went on.

During Reagan's visit, the three of them made their planned trip to Disney World. On the drive back to Jacksonville, Mama and Dad planned to eat at a very nice restaurant. However, to accommodate Reagan's childlike finicky eating, they offered to stop and let him get a McDonald burger, if he would like. He said, "That's terrific."

They got the burger and headed on down the road.

Reagan took one bite and turned up his nose. “I don’t want this hamburger.”

Dad grabbed the sandwich and instructed Mama to open up the passenger side window. With one quick motion, he threw the hamburger across the Cadillac’s white interior and out the opening.

No one said a word, as they went on to the restaurant. At the restaurant, the Maitre D’ said, “Three for lunch?”

“Oh no, only two.” Mama nodded to Reagan and continued, “He is not having lunch.”

When Mama and Dad’s meal came, they began to eat. Graciously, the waiter brought warm brown bread. Now, Mama knew that Reagan didn’t like brown bread, but she offered him some anyway. To their amazement he ate it.

After they arrived home, Mama stood in the kitchen, thinking what to fix for their evening meal. “Reagan, if I make ‘Dottie McNuggets,’ are you going to eat them?”

“Yes, ma’am,” Reagan said with a teasing smile. “Because, if I don’t eat them, you’ll throw them in the ocean.”

Mama was a fun person. She wasn’t intent on teaching lessons to her grandchildren, but when one popped up, she didn’t miss the opportunity. Without question, her grandkids knew that they were loved by a very special grandmother.

Mama was now under the care of two endocrinologists for her diabetes, plus the cardiologist. Within the past year, she had dropped two dress sizes without trying. An ever-present pain plagued her randomly throughout her body. Mama’s auburn hair began to fade in color and thin out. What was left became brittle instead of silky. “I’m hurting,” Mama kept telling her doctors. “Where is this pain coming from?”

Frustrated by her doctors and needing pain relief, Mama turned to Dr. Horsley, a chiropractor. He took a set of baseline x-rays, then began spinal adjustments. At last, someone and something was helping.

Through a self examination, Mama found a painful, finger-thick, four-inch long ridge under her left arm.

"A muscle is inflamed and causing your discomfort," one doctor told her.

"It's a fatty deposit," another offered.

"It can't be cancer," all agreed. "Early cancer is not painful. It must be your diabetes."

Each time Mama went for mammograms, she told the technician, "Be very careful how you read these. I am in some difficulty and I don't know exactly what it is." Every mammogram came back negative.

On her next visit to Dr. Montgomery, Mama showed him the ridge under her arm. Confident that this had nothing to do with her diabetes and unable to diagnose her problem, he sent her to a cancer surgeon.

The surgeon felt along the ridge under Mama's arm. "I can assure you this is not cancer," he pronounced. "Just don't worry about it. You wouldn't have pain if it were cancer, and there is no need for a biopsy." End of exam, and still no answers. Mama lived through the next three years, unaware of the malady destroying her body.

"Look at me," Mama said, six months after finding a new family care doctor, Douglas Pennington. "What's wrong with me? I'm losing weight. Where is this pain coming from?"

Dr. Pennington listened to Mama carefully, then ran a battery of tests. All the reports came back negative. The mystery still remained.

Then, one unusual Sunday morning when Dad was home, Mama went in to shower. As she stepped into the stall, her left leg gave way. Mama grabbed the door frame to break her fall, as she did the splits.

Dad heard Mama crashing around. "Dottie? Are you all right?"

"I don't think I broke anything." Tears were streaming down her cheeks. "But, there's shooting pain in my back and neck."

Dad checked her over, then helped Mama to bed.

"Gene, I think I need to see the chiropractor, Dr. Horsely. I know it's Sunday, but maybe he can give me a treatment to help with this pain."

When Dad phoned Dr. Horsley, he agreed to meet them at his office that afternoon. Since Mama hadn't been in for a while, her x-rays were almost three years old. The doctor took another set before beginning treatment. Mama and Dad waited together for Dr. Horsley's return.

"Miss Dottie," Dr. Horsley's face was more serious than Mama had ever seen it. "I can't give you an adjustment. There's something on your x-ray that concerns me. I think you need to see Dr. Pennington."

As Mama got dressed, the doctor took Dad in to look at the x-rays. "You get her to Dr. Pennington in the morning and have him call me."

Bright and early the next morning, I took Mama to Dr. Pennington's office. By now her pain was even more severe. "This can't possibly be cancer, can it?" Mama quizzed the doctor.

With her back to Dr. Pennington, Mama was unable to see his face. "I don't think so," he said, "but let's do an MRI anyway." He looked me in the eyes. We both knew there was something more.

I went out to the receptionist. "The MRI is scheduled for next week," she reported.

"No, no, no," I said. "We're going to have to do something better than that. Let's check with Humana Hospital and see when we can get her in there." Amazingly enough, Mama's MRI was scheduled for Thursday. Dad had to be out of town, so Tim canceled a long-planned hunting trip to take Mama for her test. Then, a few hours later, they decided to do a bone scan the next day.

Dad was back in town to go with Mama and me for the bone scan. It was an all-day event. Finally, at five o'clock they called the three of us to talk with Dr. Pennington. The results were in.

When Dr. Pennington entered the examination room, he was pale as a ghost. One of my nurse friends later told me he had stood in the hall crying for more than twenty minutes before he came in to see us. "Dorothy, you do have cancer," he declared.

I don't think it was my imagination, but the silence lasted

about five minutes. Dad's eyes blinked as he fought the tears. Mama openly cried. "This can't be happening to me. My people don't die of cancer. They have heart attacks and just drop dead. Besides, I'm only fifty-nine."

Dr. Pennington found his voice. "I don't understand what has happened to you. I've gone over and over your records for red flags. I don't find anything I missed."

All this time, I felt as if I were looking through a window and observing the others in the room. It wasn't until this moment that I became a part of what was happening. I could stand it no longer and asked, "How bad is it?"

"It's very bad. The cancer is everywhere." I heard Mama take in a deep breath and hold it.

With hesitation, Mama inquired, "How much time do I have?"

"Well," Dr. Pennington paused. "It's really hard to say."

"I know you're just guessing," Mama persisted, "but what do you think?"

"I would say about three months." With that, Dad closed his eyes.

Having made appointments with an oncologist, we got in the car. All of us were in a state of shock and Mama's sobs increased. "Honey," Dad said, "don't cry."

His redheaded gal emphatically said, "I'm going to cry, you're going to cry. We're all going to cry, so just let me cry."

"Okay, honey, you just go ahead and cry."

"And another thing, there are to be no secrets. Do y'all understand that? No secrets about my cancer."

It wasn't but a few hours before the whole family was informed of Mama's condition.

We went back to Mama and Dad's house and I picked up my Blazer. I had held together pretty well until now. But as I rounded the corner from their house, I stopped the vehicle. As if I erupted from inside out, screams and cries of "Why her?" poured from me. I knew right then that I needed to talk to someone. I went home and called my dear friend, Melanie Carstarphen. Not only did she listen to me, but she cried with me.

On Monday, Mama, Dad and I took all of the recent tests to the oncologist assigned to us by our HMO insurance organization. We had heard he was a fine Christian man.

He patted Mama's arm assuringly. "Bless your heart, Mrs. Williams. This is pretty bad, isn't it?"

"Doctor," Dad asked, as we followed him into the hall and out of Mama's earshot. "Just how bad is it? How long does she have?"

"Oh, I'd say three, maybe six months, at the most."

"Will you do radiation on her?" I heard Dad ask.

"Absolutely not. Her cancer is too advanced."

"How about chemotherapy?"

"W-e-l-l," the doctor pondered. "We'll probably start that in, oh, five-or-six weeks."

Oh no, my thoughts screamed. *That's half the life she has left!* With heavy feet, I dragged myself back into the exam room. *If I feel like this*, I thought, *what must Mama feel like*? I managed a smile as I helped Mama dress. Neither of us spoke.

With another appointment set in two weeks, we headed down the elevator of the medical center. "Well," Mama said. "I don't think he's going to help me fight the cancer. It sounds like, to me, he's just going to maintain me while I die."

In silence, we walked to the car. When all the doors were closed, I said, "Look, Mama, will you do something for me?"

"What?"

"Will you get a second opinion? You see, Mama," I was almost out of breath from panic, "I have a friend whose mother died last year. But she lived a long time after a very bad diagnosis. They believe it's because her doctor's a Fellow from the M.D. Anderson clinic in Houston."

Mama considered my request. "Well, that might be something we ought to do. I've heard an awful lot of good stuff about M.D. Anderson over the years."

To people from Houston, M.D. Anderson was like a household name. The doctors there, along with those at Sloan-Kettering, pioneered cancer research. I knew that a Fellow received a constant flow of the newest oncological information.

Plus an open door to receive fresh data about Mama's specific case.

"Mama," I relayed, "actually, I've already found our second opinion doctor." *Lord*, I prayed while talking, *don't let her back out now*. "I phoned my nurse friend to find the best doctor for you. I've already made an appointment with him for you in the morning. Will you just go and see what he says?"

"Okay."

When we arrived the next morning, Dad handed Dr. Mahajin the exact same test results that the previous oncologist had. First, Dr. Mahajin, a man of East Indian descent, took a brief history of the diagnosis, as well as any other medical conditions. Then he gathered up all of the tests we had brought and left the examination room.

In a few moments, Dad got on his knees and began to pray. "Dear Heavenly Father, we come to You for Your wisdom. We really don't know which way to go. The doctor we saw yesterday is a Christian, and although we would like Dorothy to be treated by a Christian doctor, we don't know if that's what You would have us do. Lord, we don't think this doctor is a Christian. But, Lord, if this is the doctor that You have for my dear Dorothy, we pray that You will make it clear, because we're giving her care to You. In Jesus' name. Amen."

"Mrs. Williams," Dr. Mahajin's words were kind but direct. "There are a couple of areas that I am very concerned about. There is a tumor on the spine. If left untreated, you most likely will become paralyzed."

My breath caught. *Why had the other doctor not mentioned paralysis?* As I reached for Mama's hand, I realized how cold mine was. Dad's hand rested on Mama's arm. Both of them kept their eyes on Dr. Mahajin. His voice sounded as if he were on the far side of a tunnel instead of just across the room.

"Also," the doctor continued, "your left femur, the thigh bone, has a very large hole in it. If your leg should break, it would have to be amputated. You might think about going into a wheelchair for a while."

Mama and Dad sat looking at each other, letting the doctor's words digest. *Why,* I wondered, *didn't the other doctor say any of this*?

Dad's words broke into my thoughts, "Do you want to do radiation?"

"Yes, but you must understand that even with radiation to the femur or the tumor on the spine, it may not correct the problem. But, yes, there are several advantages in doing radiation."

"When?" Dad inquired.

"Today."

"What about chemotherapy," I chimed in.

"Absolutely," Dr. Mahajin answered.

"When?" Dad again inquired.

"Immediately. Today, if possible."

I could tell right away that Dad was feeling real good about Dr. Mahajin. He turned to Mama and asked, "What would you like to do, Dorothy?"

"Let's get on with it. I don't have a minute to spare."

With that, Dr. Mahajin picked up the phone and began issuing orders.

"Mrs. Williams," the nurse steered a wheelchair toward us, "let me show you how to protect your leg as you get in and out of this chair."

Suddenly, my heart flip-flopped as Mama maneuvered herself into the wheelchair. Always a strong woman, I now saw her as a frail invalid. Dad's face mirrored my thoughts.

Mama looked at the nurse, "I guess I'm all set."

"Hang on," I tried joking. "We'll see what kind of a driver I am, Dad." I reached for his arm, patted it, and said, "You may have to rescue us."

Thankful for something to do, Dad and I wheeled Mama across the street. Here, radiation technicians soon had ink-colored dots on her neck and left upper leg. These landmarks guided rays intended to kill cancerous growths, while allowing protection of healthy areas.

I fought to choke back my real feelings, to put on a joyful face. Right now it was real hard to find something positive in all the negatives. *How could this be happening?* The thoughts whirled in my brain. *Mama had gone for all her check ups, seen all these doctors and even been hospitalized three times. How could she have fallen through the cracks of the medical system?*

I wondered how I was going to survive without her. My mama was one person who loved me unconditionally. I didn't want to blow spiritual smoke or recite a pat answer, like "God's in control." All I could remember about my mama's teaching was that there's always something positive in any sea of negatives. And that the goodness of this situation was that I might become more like Christ. But right now, I was angry, and we had declared war on Mama's cancer. The first battle was under our belts. Somehow, being in action gave us hope.

On the way home from the doctor, I could tell that something was bothering Dad. Even without Mama's illness, he had a lot of pressure on him. The Luther Rice Board of Regents had voted to move the seminary from Jacksonville to Atlanta, Georgia. Mama and Dad had moved to a lovely condo closer to the school but were expecting to go with the seminary. Mama had made many moves in her life and was not about to miss this one. They had been expecting to move in a few months.

Dad also had a lot of meetings lined up, including an evangelistic crusade in Nigeria for which he was due to leave right away. "Dottie," he asked, when we got back home, "what do you want me to do about my meetings?"

"So many decisions have to be made in the next while," Mama sighed. "I've never asked you to stay home, but I really think I might need your help this time. Could you make some other arrangements about Nigeria?"

Almost at that moment, their doorbell rang. Dad opened the door to friends Ben and Nita Rogers. Ben had traveled with Dad on nearly every overseas crusade. It was Ben who had described Mama as a cross between the famous missionary, Lottie Moon, and the celebrated actress, Lucille Ball.

"Doc," Ben addressed Dad, "we know that you've received some bad news. I've come to tell you that I will take the group to Nigeria for you. You need to be here with Dottie."

Mama and Dad agreed. All we could do was marvel at how

God had already worked this out. And God blessed richly in Nigeria, with a great in-gathering of new believers during the crusade.

"What can we do, Mama?" Randy and Tim asked in turn. Randy was now pastor of the First Baptist Church of Tampa, Florida. Tim was a full-time evangelist. I was busy with my counseling practice.

We knew Mama's radiation and chemo could last for up to three months. She would be in the wheelchair until the treatments were completed or she was unable to continue.

"Mama," I said, "you're going to need someone to take you for treatments and help care for you. Would you like for me to take off from my practice for a few months?"

"No, indeed," came her ready reply to all of us. "All of you, please, back off." This was the spunky Mama we knew, and she did not appreciate our hovering. "Let me do all the things I can do, as long as I can do them."

"Mama," Randy spoke for Tim and me, too. "We love you and we want to do this your way."

"Randy," she said with determination, "You have lives to touch through the church you pastor. Keep doing what God has called you to do. Tim," she continued, "think of all the people who won't come to the Lord if you're not out there preaching.

"You know," Mama's voice broke slightly, "this cancer could get real hairy before we're through with it. Each of you may have to come from wherever you are and help me. But, right now, let me do what I can do. Let me live, and I want you to live. I've spent lots of years," Mama continued, "teaching you how to live. Now it seems I'm going to teach you how to die. There will be no secrets," she again emphasized. "We will all—including the grandchildren—know everything I know about my illness."

The news of Mama's terminal illness literally spread around the world. Hundreds wrote that they were praying. Among the many who came to visit her were two of her dearest, long-standing women friends. Tears filled Mama's eyes when she saw them enter. No words were necessary as their comforting arms wrapped around each other. For a couple of hours, they sat and laughed together, recalling God's goodness to each of them.

"This is not a time to be sad." Mama smiled as she spoke. "I've had the very best that God offers. My husband loves me dearly, and we're still sweethearts—as you both are with your husbands.

"Please don't feel sorry for me," Mama continued. "I know that when I get to heaven, throngs of people from all over the world will be there because they heard God's message through the preaching of my husband and sons and my daughter's songs and testimony. It's like I've had a special, tall chair from which I've been able to watch God work and move. How many women get to do that?"

Things began to fall into place as God provided Rachel Camp to help Mama with cleaning and shopping. Many friends volunteered rides for appointments.

Mama handled the wheelchair well and never seemed to resent it. But it was a constant reminder to me that she wasn't going to be around much longer. As one of the few people who saw Mama undressed, it was sometimes hard to look at her. There was no escaping the deterioration of her cancer-ravaged body.

Some days, she seemed so weak. I had known her as such a youthful, vivacious, full-of-energy woman. Now, her strength was failing and the shadow of death was creeping over her horizon. With Dad gone so much, Mama was the one person I had always been able to count on to love me. The idea of her being gone, frankly frightened the starch out of me.

In fact, the day after Mama received her diagnosis, I called a counselor. Even though I was a counselor, I wanted professional help dealing with the pain of losing Mama.

My family knew I was going for counseling. While Mama did not feel the need to go herself, she encouraged me. I used my half dozen sessions to work through my grief; to cry and purge my hurt. Because I dealt with my own feelings quickly, I was able to help her more. And I began to pray, *God, prove that You are God and this is part of your handiwork.*

Dad, Tim, Randy and I were outraged that Mama's problem had not been diagnosed sooner. Convinced that she had been the victim of medical negligence, we talked to a lawyer friend and were told we could probably win a multimillion dollar suit. We went to Mama with this opinion.

"Let me consider it and seek the Lord's guidance," Mama delayed. She realized that all the doctors who cared for her would have to be named in a suit. Most of those doctors were as astonished as we were when advanced cancer was found. They were Mama's friends and wanted the best for her. She did not want to harm them.

"I do not have energy for a suit," Mama decided. "I don't want my mind or thoughts cluttered with a lawsuit. The energy I have, I want to put into trying to live as long as I can live. If we're going to win against this cancer, I need all my energy for fighting it. I haven't lived my life fighting people, and I'm not going to end my life doing so."

Mama seemed to always get her priorities right.

During this time three-and-a-half-year-old Brittney's faith was something to behold. On days when Tim, Joy or I took her with us around the city, she sought out prayers.

"Do you know my grandmommie?" Brittney's blonde curls bounced as she focused on the person's face.

"Yes," the acquaintance would smile at this pensive child. "I know your grandmother."

"Then, you know my grandmommie's got this big old cancer?"

"Yes, I know."

"Well," Brittney would stress, "you need to pray for my grandmommie. Pray that God will kill her big old cancer."

"Oh, yes." Who could turn down such a plea? "I'll pray for your grandmommie."

And Brittney followed her own advice. She got down on her knees and prayed for Mama and her big old cancer every night.

One bright sunshiny day Brittney and I were driving across town. Suddenly, from nowhere, Brittney asked, "Is Grandmommie going to die?"

"Yes, Brittney, someday. But not today."

"Do you think when she dies, that she'll see Jesus?" Brittney's little nose curled up as she inquired.

"Yes, ma'am, I surely do."

"Do you think she'll tell Jesus 'hi' for me?" She spoke as if Jesus was her very best friend and she had known him a long, long time.

"Tell you what, Brittney. Why don't you talk to Grandmommie about this, and I'll bet she'll take care of it."

Before Mama's chemo caused her hair to fall out, she and I had gone to a wig shop. We giggled our way through picking out one hair wig that matched her once-auburn hair, as well as a blonde one.

Now, as the family gathered for Christmas, Mama sat in her wheelchair. Eleven-year-old Reagan came in and walked all the way around her, looking Mama—and her wig—over very closely.

Mama's head followed him around. "Well, what do you think?"

"Grandmother," Reagan said, without any hesitation. "It looks almost like the original to me."

"You know," Mama told us later, "It won't be long before the children will want to see me without my wig."

"Dottie," Dad asked, "aren't you afraid it might be too much for them?"

"If they're curious enough to ask, then they can take it."

"Grandmommie," Brittney asked, the very next day with Judson and Reagan beside her. "What do you look like without your wig?"

"Well," Mama returned, "you've all seen bald men. Right?"

"Yeah," Judson said, as all three heads nodded.

"Well," she shrugged, "I look just like them." Mama's body language told them it was no big deal.

"Oh, yeah," Reagan piped.

"Here, I'll show you." Mama lifted her wig off as three pairs of eyes watched. Brittney, Judson and Reagan walked around her to see from several angles.

"You're right, Grandmommie," Brittney said. "You do look like a bald man." Then they hugged Mama and ran out to play.

God is full of blessings, I reflected. It seemed impossible to ignore the memory of that three-year-old, bald-headed Dottie who had been teased by other children, but was taught by her parents that she was wonderful. The self-confidence and love her parents instilled in her held firm now that she was a bald-headed chemo patient. She still knew her value was beyond that of gold.

Mama, of course, was not able to get out and shop. Almost every time I stopped in to see her, the TV was tuned to QVC or HSC, the shopping channels. Since Mama knew her products, she was able to spot bargains and order them for herself or us. We all teased her about her home shopping.

On Christmas Eve, all the family gathered to open our presents. We were about to the end of the gift giving when Randy suddenly stood up and got our attention. "Now, y'all, we need to stop right now. We just need to stop right now."

"Why, Randy?" Tim asked.

"What do you mean?" the grandchildren chimed in.

We all looked at Randy as if he had lost his mind. But I noticed a smile on Mama's face. She was very familiar with Randy's dry sense of humor. So she was ready for the punchline.

"We need to get on our knees, right here." Randy emphasized every word sounding like a stereotyped TV evangelist. "And thank God for the TV shopping channels. If it weren't for TV shopping, we wouldn't have any Christmas at all this year." Of course, all of us nearly doubled over laughing.

Reagan and Judson were disappointed about not receiving one particular gift for Christmas. After seeing Mama, they both decided they wanted matching wheelchairs. Since that was not in the wind for family gift-giving, they took the opportunity to learn how to lay rubber with Grandmother's wheelchair.

Mama laughed a lot about the watch she gave Randy that year. When asked for gift suggestions, Christa told Mama, "Randy would like a new watch. His old watch is just terrible."

Soon after that, Mama saw this nugget watch on TV. Knowing Randy had always been picky about his dress, Mama phoned Christa. "Do you think my son Randy would like a nugget watch with twenty-four diamonds?"

"Well, I suppose so."

"Ask him. They've got one on TV. It's a $250 watch and they're selling it for $69. If he wants one, I'll get it."

Well, the watch looked great on him. And it really did have twenty-four little diamonds around its face.

"Mama," Randy said, one day in January. "I've called to give you your giggle for the day."

"What is it?"

"Well, I was up at one of the clubs, having lunch with some men from the church. Near the end of our meal, one of them leaned over and said, 'Pastor, that's a good looking watch'."

" 'Thank you,' I said. `My mama gave it to me.'

" 'Well, I certainly hope you have it insured.'

"I kind of mumbled a little bit," Randy told Mama, "then turned the conversation in another direction. But when I got in the car, I nearly died laughing. Insure Mama's $69 watch?"

In addition to everything else, Tim and Joy were about to have a new baby. They asked Mama to care for Brittney when their second child was born. They wanted Mama to bring Brittney to the hospital so she could welcome her new sister. When Mama looked at her calendar and realized she would be in the middle of taking a cancer treatment, her first reaction was to say, "No. I just can't cope with Brittney on top of the chemo. I can't do it."

But after some thought, Mama decided she didn't want to miss out on such a special experience.

The day Ashlyn arrived, Mama and Brittney buddied around.

"Now, Grandmommie, you have just about finished all your Andy Mouse chemo treatments?"

"Yes, sweetie. I've just about finished the Adriamycin."

"Well, I want to know how your hair is." Mama's hair hadn't been talked about in a long time, but Brittney remembered her saying it would grow back, once she finished her treatments.

"Well, it's growing. It's not very much, but it's growing a little bit."

"Grandmommie, I want to see your new hair."

"All right," Mama said, as she took off her wig. She hadn't mentioned that it was coming back grayish black instead of auburn. Brittney frowned slightly as she walked around, studying Mama. Just then Dad called. Realizing Brittney was there, Dad asked to talk to her.

Papa Doc was her special name for Dad, because she's heard so many people call him Doc. "Papa Doc," she said, "I've been looking at Grandmommie's hair."

"So what do you think?"

Dad exploded in laughter as she said, "I think we're going to have to paint it."

Mama took Brittney with her to the doctor's office. Since she had gone with Mama before, the treatment room did not frighten Brittney. In fact, she looked at the nurses and said, "Now, y'all must hurry with Grandmommie's Andy Mouse treatment, `cause I'm getting a baby sister today."

"You are?" the nurses said. "Well, we'd better hurry, then." And they scurried around, getting Mama's pouch for continuous IV chemo changed so she and Brittney could beat it down to the hospital.

During the hour-and-a-half before Ashlyn was born, Brittney and Mama sat in the waiting room, talking about sisters.

"You know, Grandmommie, I talk to 'Sissy' every day."

"Do you really? Every day?"

"Yes. Everyday I get up and tell her good morning."

"Well, if you talk to 'Sissy' every day, she's going to know your voice when she's born."

"She will? She really will?"

"Yes. I'm sure she will."

About then, a nurse called the two of them to Joy's room. "Hey, Brittney," her smiling dad said.

"Come see who's here," Joy added.

Mama took Brittney's hand and they crossed to the bed where Joy and the just-cleaned-up baby lay. "Oh!" Brittney's face broke into a smile. "Can I hold her?"

Just like magic, Ashlyn turned her head toward Brittney's

voice. Brittney wheeled around and looked at Mama with excitement in her tiny blue eyes. "She really does know my voice, Grandmommie. She really does."

"Well, of course she knows your voice," Mama said.

Joy said, "Go over to the recliner and sit very still." Tim took the brand new bundle and laid her in Brittney's lap.

"Sissy, Sissy," Brittney sang as Ashlyn's little head flopped in her direction. "I'm so glad you're here. I've waited for you a long, long time. I'll love you all my life. I'll never, never, never throw you away. You'll be my Sissy all my life."

"It was the sweetest, most precious thing," Mama said many times afterwards. "What if I had missed this because I was taking chemo? I'd have missed seeing those little grandchildren meet for the first time."

During the summer of Ashlyn's birth, all of the grandchildren except Reagan spent time with Mama. He was a pitcher on his ball team, and had to wait until their games were played before making the trip from Tampa to Jacksonville. Finally, Randy called Mama, and said, "Reagan wants to come if it will be all right." Of course, Mama was thrilled to know her twelve-year-old grandson still wanted to come visit.

After he arrived, Mama said, "Grandmother's sorry that we can't go do all the things that we used to do."

"But, Grandmother," Reagan said, showing his understanding of her condition, "isn't it wonderful that we did get to do all those things."

Reagan left Mama in the clouds, saying, "I wonder, I just wonder what God's going to do with that boy."

Mama believed God had His hand on all her grandchildren, just as she'd believed that way about us.

Chapter Fifteen

Mama, the Conqueror

AS TIME WENT ON, we realized radiation had shrunk the neck tumor but did nothing to Mama's leg tumor. In March, Dr. Mahajin recommended surgery. He wanted a rod placed in Mama's leg to strengthen it. He was trying to give her as much quality of life as he could, and get her out of the wheelchair. Thinking that Mama's time left could be nearly over, I began calling friends.

One of the members of First Baptist Church, Jacksonville was a well-respected orthopedic surgeon. But he couldn't get to Mama for two weeks. We could not wait. Of course, people around the world were praying for Mama. That's the only thing that could explain the peace we had during this time.

Then I found Dr. Buckingham who made time to see Mama right away. He blustered into the examination room and they hit it off at once. Mama nicknamed him "the old sea captain." He turned out to be a fantastic orthopedic surgeon.

Surgery was scheduled at Jacksonville's Baptist Hospital, with an expected five-to-six day stay.

Reagan and Judson talked with Mama on the phone. "Grandmother, we'll be praying for your operation."

"You know what they're planning to do to me, don't you?"

"What, Grandmother?"

"They're going to put a metal rod in my leg and hold it together with bolts and screws."

"Really?" The boys giggled with Mama. "Are they really?"

Mama and I took care of the admission procedures and she was in her room at the appointed time. Dad flew in from a revival on the morning of surgery. Randy came from Tampa.

The anesthesiologist I requested was assigned to Mama. Because of her cardiac history and because we understood this was a painful procedure, we asked Dr. Kramp to consider an epidural anesthetic which would reduce the pain after surgery. Contrary to the opinion of her nurse, he readily agreed and inserted the pain killer through a long tube in Mama's back.

Dr. Mahajin looked in on Mama during the surgery, even though Mama was admitted under Dr. Buckingham's care. Dr. Mahajin came out to assure us, "She's doing okay."

The surgery took a little longer than expected, so Mama asked Dr. Buckingham if she could call us in the waiting area. "I'm just fine," she said. "I was afraid you'd be worried. This is a crazy bunch in here, and I'm making sure they get both legs the same length. I'll see you in a little while."

Awake throughout the surgery, Mama returned to her room alert and calm. "You should have been there," she said. Then blow by blow, she proceeded to tell about Dr. Buckingham blustering to the nurses and making sure he had the right length rod. Her smile nearly broke her face as she showed us the dressing on her left leg. "You should have seen Dr. Buckingham and Dr. Mahajin almost dancing in the hall because the surgery went so well. The epidural worked great—I don't feel any pain. And, Dr. Buckingham said that by tomorrow, I'll be walking on this leg."

"Oh, Mama, that's great," Randy and I chorused as Dad gave Mama a hug.

Just then, the frowning nurse who had already told Mama that an epidural anesthesia was inappropriate for her surgery, entered the room. "All of you need to get out of here. She needs her rest."

Mama looked at the nurse like, *I'm perfectly capable of telling them when to leave*. However, not wanting to raise a fuss, we took judicious turns sitting with Mama after that.

With the dosed epidural, Mama stayed pain free and slept through the night.

Dr. Buckingham hustled in the next morning and ordered, "Girl, get up and walk."

"You're sure I should do this?" Mama straightened the pink

colored scarf-bonnet on her hairless head, while searching the doctor's face. When he just stood there waiting, she scooted to the bed's edge. Dr. Buckingham handed her the walker. Mama let her legs dangle while keeping her IV line untangled. Then with hardly a grimace, she pulled herself up tall. "All right, we'll give it a try."

"It won't break," the doctor assured. He beamed as she took one step, then two. "You just keep walking on it."

Mama paused to regain her composure after walking across the room. "Dr. Buckingham, this is unbelievable. I don't even hurt. How can I begin to thank you for what you've done?"

"There is no surgery in the world that I would rather do than this one." His eyes sparkled and a smile split his face. "It is great to see people get up and walk again."

Mama did so well after surgery that Dr. Kramp soon switched her from the epidural to pain pills, and Dr. Buckingham decided to dismiss her a couple of days early. Still a little nauseated after surgery, Mama had not eaten a full meal yet.

Suddenly, the grumpy nurse charged in, armed with a tray of Cajun chicken ala king and sugary foods. We'd already struggled with her over many things, including the treatment of Mama's diabetic condition. When Mama's sugars were elevated this nurse had insisted she drink a Coke Classic. Mama was a well-informed diabetic. She flatly refused, saying, "All I need is a diabetic coma caused by another medical *faux pas*." Now the nurse had the audacity to say, "Mrs. Williams, you have to eat all of this before I can let you leave the hospital."

"I do?" Mama stared at the food.

"Yes, ma'am," the nurse barked as she left the room.

"Sandra," Mama wrinkled her nose. "If I eat this horrible stuff, I'll be in the hospital for the rest of this week."

Looking back, I think we were so angry with the medical profession that this nurse could have said, "Boo!" and we would have jumped all over her. But she was the only caregiver at that time who was acting unprofessionally.

Mama's determined look met mine. We did not speak, but each of us knew the other had had enough. Mama and I drew the line: From this time forward, we would accept only good medical and nursing care. As human beings we expected to be treated with respect, and wanted no further abuse from the system. Those in medicine are not God Almighty. Mama had the cancer to prove it. Mama picked up her roll and threw it across the room into the trash can. I carried the entree into the bathroom and emptied it into the commode. One flush took care of the evidence.

A few minutes later the grumpy nurse came back and inspected Mama's tray. "I see you have eaten. I guess you can leave now."

While Mama completed her dismissal routine, I went down to the nursing office and asked for the director. "I've never done this before," I began, when she agreed to see me. "But I want you to know what we have gone through while my mama was a patient here." I filled her in on specific episodes of what I considered unprofessional behavior by the nurse. "I don't plan to do anything more about it, but I know that the only way you know what goes on in the units is if people tell you. By the way, why do you have a nurse who was fired from another hospital treating my mother?"

"Uh . . uh," the woman stuttered. "How do you know that?"

"That's not the question. The question is how could you allow my mother to be treated by such an unqualified nurse."

We were not angry, we were just taking charge. From that point on, we took ownership of Mama's care.

Dr. Mahajin got a surprise the next day when he discovered Mama had been discharged. He had planned to have a Port-a-Cath inserted before Mama's dismissal. This device is great for cancer patients because the veins become very fragile as a result of the chemo. Leaving the catheter in place almost eliminates additional needle sticks for white blood counts and treatments. Since Mama was already at home, Dr. Mahajin arranged for her to return to the hospital as an outpatient.

When Mama came in, she did a double-take at seeing the doctor assigned to treat her. He was the one who had done her biopsies at the beginning. Mama had named him "Dr. Bedside

Manner" because he had failed his "bedside manner" course in med school. "Or maybe," she had quipped, "he was absent that day." Nonetheless, after the biopsy he had told her there was no hope.

"Well, surprise, surprise!" Mama squealed. "As you can see, I'm still alive." Mama started laughing. The doctor joined her. I don't know what his thoughts were, but Mama said that his bedside manner improved immensely.

When the nurses checked Mama over, they discovered she was running a low-grade fever. They rescheduled her for the next day. "Be here by seven a.m.," the nurse instructed. When the fever persisted, they booked her for another visit. Again, she had to be at the hospital by seven in the morning. Finally, on the third try, Mama was fever-free, and the Port-a-Cath was inserted. By now, she and the surgeon were joking with each other.

A week later, Mama returned to Dr. Bedside Manner for stitch removal. After a few minutes, their conversation turned serious. The doctor looked her dead in the eye. "The oncologist who referred you to me is a friend of mine. I was wondering why he is no longer your treating physician?"

"Because I would have been dead by now," Mama answered curtly. "He was the first oncologist I saw and I didn't feel that he was going to treat my cancer aggressively."

Silence surrounded them as the doctor pulled out the last stitch, washed his hands, and left the room. Mama dressed and walked out into the hallway.

"Well," Dr. Bedside Manner said, smiling and wrapping his arm around Mama's shoulder, "I'm glad you're still alive, Dorothy. If there's anything I can do for you, don't hesitate to let me know."

As Mama left his office, she winked at me and said, "Maybe he wasn't absent that day in med school after all."

As word of Mama's illness continued to spread, phone calls and notes came from all directions. Many Christians seemed to expect Mama and Dad to be crushed by the cancer diagnosis. And they seemed bothered by the fact that they weren't.

"Don't they know us better than that?" Mama wondered

aloud, shocked at their flawed logic. "Why would we be destroyed? I don't understand why God has allowed the cancer, but He has. He is still the same sovereign God as always. We have been, and we still are, in His hands."

Then, she caught wind of the Christian community's criticism of Dad for continuing his revival commitments. She could not understand this judgment from Christians. It was almost the last straw.

Mama called in some friends. "This has been totally my decision that Gene continue preaching and traveling for the seminary. People won't buy it when Gene tells them, so I need your help in getting out the truth. You know," Mama asked rhetorically, "what will happen if he stops preaching? Word will get out that he's no longer holding meetings, and he'll never get back to where he is now. It will be hard enough for Gene to lose me. I don't want him to lose his ministry, too. A man that God has called to preach has got to preach."

"Of course," the friends agreed, "we'll help."

And it worked. Wherever they went, when our situation came up, Mama's friends told others that Dad continued to preach and travel because it was what Mama wanted. Naturally our family did the same thing.

Mama and I talked alone one day. "Mama," I said, "you've got to be fair with Dad. You've got to take time to prepare him to live without you."

"I know." Tears brimmed her eyes as she nodded. "I know, Sandee. I've been trying to figure out what to do."

I was sure that her thoughts matched mine. Dad hadn't done laundry or gone grocery shopping for a long time. Mama always cared for Dad, almost to a fault. She laundered his clothes, picked up his dry cleaning, packed his suitcase, took care of house, car, and family. Any need that Dad expressed, Mama took care of—almost before the words were out of his mouth. But it was all done because she loved Dad and wanted his time at home to be spent with her. Mama always figured people were coming to Christ in Dad's meetings because she did laundry or got the car tuned, instead of leaving it for her preacher husband to do. To her, this was not a job or something a wife should do but what God had called her to do as part of our outreach.

"Gene, you've got to go preach," I heard her tell Dad so many times. It wasn't that he doubted God's call, he just wanted to stay in the home-nest Mama had created. "You've got to go. That's what God wants you to do."

"Mama," Tim used to joke, "I think, when I get married, I'll be able to get my own ice water."

"That's fine, son, but I'll get your dad's as long as I can."

I ached all over for Mama and Dad later, as she told me about one of Dad's first shopping trips in some forty years.

It was a Saturday morning near the end of the year. Mama sat in the car while Dad went into a large supermarket for a few groceries.

Dodging children and other shoppers in this still-new world, he finally found what he needed. Then, ready to check out, he got into line and unloaded his goods on the counter.

"Sir," the checkout girl loudly snapped, "you have too many items to be in this lane."

"Oh, I didn't realize. I beg your pardon." By now others stood behind Dad and heads of shoppers in the aisles were turned in his direction. "Shall I move?"

"Well," the cashier sighed dramatically, obviously trying to embarrass him. "I'll check you out today. But, next time, please look before you get in line."

Mama said that when he came out, she knew something had gone wrong. "What happened?" she asked.

Tears filled Dad's eyes. Their ride home was quiet.

Then as they put things away in the kitchen, their eyes met. "Oh, Dottie." This was Dad's time to grieve over the prospect of losing Mama. "There are people smoking, drinking and abusing their bodies in so many other ways. Why don't they have cancer? Why you?"

"We spent the rest of that day crying and holding each other," Mama told me later. Her smile offset moist eyes. "We had so looked forward to being together during these years, that it never occurred to us we wouldn't be. We don't know why God has allowed this, and we may never know. But we know that He knows, and He's given us a peace about it. The Lord never promised that serving and following Him would guarantee no troubles. This just happens to be ours."

I wiped my eyes and smiled at my incredible mother. Suddenly, I saw myself as a third grader and Mama confronting Mrs. Grouch and the principal. I knew I couldn't just let this incident slide by.

The following Friday I met with the store manager. "I really believe your cashier's attitude toward my father last Saturday was inappropriate. There are men out here who have lost their wives, and they are trying to discover how to function in this world. Men who haven't been in a store for forty or fifty years. Now, I realize she was young, but surely this can't be the policy of the store to be more concerned about a line than about a person."

"I'm sorry that this happened, and thank you for telling me. Trust me, our policy is to be more interested in a person. And, if your father would like my assistance in any way, please let me know."

I had never in my life fought a battle for my dad, but it was obvious that this incident had bothered my mother greatly. Maybe I shouldn't have said anything to the store manager, and maybe it was said in anger. All I know is, I was awfully tired of us being kicked in the gut. I couldn't yell at the cancer. There was nothing I could do to fix the cancer. But, there was some comfort in being able to rectify one injustice our family faced. Somehow I suspect my spunky mama would have been proud of me.

Mama said later, "There are many women who get to this point in life and their husbands leave them. The wife is not able to do what she used to do, or be what she used to be. Then if she gets cancer and her body begins to decay, the husband walks away. I have been so fortunate that your dad has stood with me through this time of my life, when many men would have walked away. How sad it would be to live our lives together, through the good and the bad, then when the ugly came, to have been abandoned. I am so blessed," she mused, "to have a husband who loves me as he has." She smothered a quiet chuckle. "Why your dad, Sandee, has stood with me through thick hair and thin."

I don't think it ever crossed Dad's mind to think of leaving my mama during this time. In my counseling practice, I've heard distraught women cry over a husband's unfaithfulness. Thank God, that's one trouble my mama never had to endure.

There are many things I am not sure about in life, but this I am. My mama and my dad were best friends. They were partners, lovers, and they were sweethearts. All the way.

"Gene," Mama said, "I really do think we need to go on and move to Atlanta with the seminary."

"But, honey, all of your doctors are here, and I don't want your treatment to be held up in any way."

"Well, this is how I feel about it. It's important for me to make you a new nest before I leave. The seminary needs you at this time, and I think it will be important when I die for you to be near your support system. Besides I'm sure there are good doctors in Atlanta, as well."

So off to Atlanta my dying mama went, with two tasks at hand. To prepare a home for Dad and to find new doctors.

Our insurance company transferred us to a new HMO in the Atlanta area. We found an oncologist who gave all the right answers to Mama's interview questions. Up to this point we had kept Mama's three-inch thick packet of x-rays in our possession. When this new doctor asked for a week to examine the x-rays, I spoke up. "We'll be back in a couple of days to pick the records up. We keep them with us all the time, because they can get lost in these hospitals."

We knew from Dr. Mahajin that one guideline used in cancer treatment is, "if the pain increases, probably the cancer is active." When I took Mama to her appointment at the end of that week, she told the new doctor, "I'm having more pain in my neck and shoulders."

"Well, you have cancer. You're supposed to have pain."

When Mama asked for her x-rays back, the doctor said he was still reviewing the file.

Mama had sailed through the chemo treatments without heart problems. However, now that the chemo was finished, partial heart failure reappeared. Mama had been under a heart doctor's care since the episode in Las Vegas two years before. Now she needed a cardiologist in Atlanta. Mama's new, female, HMO primary-care doctor not only refused to refer her to a cardiologist in Atlanta, she brushed off our request for her medical file with the excuse that she couldn't put her hands on it right at the moment.

So Mama just got up, took charge of herself and found Dr. Lesser, one of the finest cardiologists in the Atlanta area. He worked very closely with Mama, allowing her to monitor herself at home. Then, after more than two months of treatment, the heart failure disappeared. Just as before, the only explanation was that God had intervened.

Each time Mama saw the new HMO oncologist, she repeated that her neck and shoulder pain was increasing. When Mama suggested more tests, the doctor told her they were unnecessary. When she asked about going back on the chemo to control the cancer, he sidestepped or avoided her. He allowed Mama no participation in her care. When we asked him if he'd found her medical file and X-ray jacket, he mumbled, "I'm not finished with them yet." We grew suspicious that they were lost, for it was obvious this doctor did not have them as a reference point.

During Mama's April, 1992 visit, I asked the doctor if he was going to try and find why the pain had increased. The doctor ignored my question by refusing to answer. As he turned to walk out the door, I called him by name, and said, "Sir, just keep in mind I am permanent, but you are temporary." As Mama left his office in tears, she said, "I don't feel safe with this doctor, Sandee. I'm afraid he is going to let the cancer grow and we won't know about it until more damage is already done."

"Why don't we go down to Jacksonville, talk to Dr. Mahajin and see if we can regroup?" I suggested. Tired of medical foot dragging and delays, we were determined to find some answers. "Another second opinion from Dr. Mahajin wouldn't hurt anything," I told Mama. "Perhaps he can help us find an M.D. Anderson Fellow in the Atlanta area."

Before the end of the day, we contacted Dr. Mahajin. He made arrangements for a new bone scan in Jacksonville the next morning.

We flew to Jacksonville to keep the appointment. After they did the scan, Dr. Mahajin came into the examination room to help us sort things out. He said that from what he could tell, the cancer had not increased. But it was very hard for him to make a comparison because he no longer had Mama's medical records to find a baseline. Even though there were no M.D. Anderson Fellows in the Atlanta area, he offered to see what he could do to get Mama settled with another oncologist. Just to see for myself, I asked if I could look in the directory that listed the M.D. Anderson Fellows. He went and got the book.

I examined the Georgia listings, and found a M.D. Anderson Fellow with offices in, of all places, Tucker and Conyers, Georgia, both suburbs of Atlanta. Dr. Mahajin immediately picked up the phone and talked to Dr. Bruce Feinberg. He gave Mama an appointment for a couple of days later.

Dr. Feinberg's smile was genuine, his handshake firm and his step decisive as he welcomed Mama and me into his office. As we talked, Mama's face relaxed. I could almost feel the same ease and trust building toward Dr. Feinberg as we had felt toward Dr. Mahajin.

Mama asked, "Do you like your mother?"

He looked at her in a query and said, "Yes. Why do you ask?"

"Well, I figure that I'm about the same age as your mother would be. And, I figure if you like her, you'll like me." Mama was feeling more and more comfortable with Dr. Feinberg.

My question was, "Why do you do this kind of medicine? Isn't it kind of depressing?"

It was obvious he had thought through this question before. "Most of the time it is not done very well. Someone needs to do it right."

After our questions, he said, "Mrs. Williams, with what Dr. Mahajin has told me and your present symptoms, I think we should get another MRI as soon as possible."

"Thank you, Dr. Feinberg," Mama said. "I—we'll—feel better once we know for sure what we are dealing with."

The first date we could get for the MRI was the end of the week. During our wait, Mama and I persisted in calling the first Atlanta oncologist's office. "We want those records," we reminded his assistant.

"Your records are at the hospital," she informed us.

We called the hospital. "No," the clerk said, "we have nothing here on Dorothy Williams' x-rays." The oncologist then claimed he had never received the x-ray jacket and files. I reminded him that I had handed them to him personally. He didn't respond. Here we were on another merry-go-round of medical ineptness.

Mama's MRI was done at four o'clock, the afternoon of Friday, May 1, at Rockdale Hospital. We felt a sense of relief because, whatever it showed, we would be back on the offensive. The phone rang. "Mrs. Williams? This is the radiologist at Rockdale Hospital. I've just talked to Dr. Feinberg. He wants you to come to the hospital immediately."

Mama said a kind of numbness settled over her, and she thought, *I was right about the cancer getting worse*. "To the hospital now? To be admitted?"

"Yes. Dr. Feinberg wants you here as soon as possible, but you are not to drive yourself."

Dad and I had already left for an evening out at a tennis tournament. Mama had insisted that we go.

Ben and Nita Rogers drove Mama to the hospital.

Dr. Feinberg later met with us and explained that, as Mama suspected, the once-radiated neck tumor had become active again. "The tumor is pressing against the spinal cord and about to sever it. You need surgery," he told Mama. "Who do you want to do the surgery?"

"Dr. Feinberg," Mama said, "we are new in Atlanta. We don't know the doctors here. You choose a surgeon that you would let operate on your spinal cord, and I'll let him operate on mine."

Then Dad spoke up. "I want Dottie to have every advantage

possible. If there's a surgeon whose skill would increase her chances by even ten percent, get him. We want whoever can do the best job."

"All right," Dr. Feinberg agreed. "We'll have to move you, because this type of surgery is not done here. When I find your surgeon, we'll decide which hospital."

After Dr. Feinberg left the room, we sat looking at each other, trying to absorb what he had said. We realized again that, even though Mama had cancer and a limited time left, we were not prepared for her death.

"Dottie," Dad broke the silence. "Do you remember that I am scheduled for a one-day revival meeting on Sunday? I should notify the church that I will not be able to come."

"That church has made great preparation, Gene. If it's at all possible, I want you to go."

"Well, Dottie, let's talk with Dr. Feinberg tomorrow to see what he has found out about the surgery. Then we can decide."

Dr. Feinberg told them that Dr. Hartman, the surgeon he wanted, would not be available until the following Tuesday. "We're working on fitting you into the operating room schedule at DeKalb Medical Center. Monday is the earliest you would be moved."

Hearing that, Mama again told Dad to go. Again, some people did not understand. Some attempted to set Dad up as the bad guy by saying, "Oh, you mean Gene's not there?"

"Well, no." Mama's face and voice registered surprise at the question. "I asked him to leave. I helped kick him out the door." She made people understand that it really was part of her philosophy, and she was not being mistreated. And, it was very freeing to the family. We were allowed to do what God wanted without unnecessary guilt.

By Sunday, word had gone out that it was very likely Mama would not survive this surgery. Mama got calls from all across the country that people were praying for her. One call came from little Brittney. Of course, Tim and Joy had prepared her for the possibility that this was the time for Grandmommie to go to be with Jesus. Brittney was weeping. "I don't want you to have an operation."

Mama wept with her, in one of those bittersweet times. "Sweetheart, I don't want to have an operation either. But, you remember when Grandmommie was in the wheel chair and couldn't walk? The doctors operated, and then I could walk around with you. We held hands and did things together. If I don't have this operation, we can't go to the beach, or walk down to the pool, or go to the mall and buy a new dress." Mama then prayed with Brittney and she stopped crying.

People Mama had known and loved for years—many in connection with Luther Rice—came to see her that Sunday before the Tuesday surgery. Some were couples she had watched grow and develop since they had small children. Now their children were in college or getting married. And, it was apparent they loved Mama. They were able to say some of the sweet things to each other that, often when it's too late, we only wish we had.

Mama said afterwards, "It was the sweetest day I think I've ever spent. I never had such peace in my life. I have absolutely no fear of the surgery."

On Monday, Mama termed the ambulance that transferred her to DeKalb "a torture chamber. Every time it hit a blade of grass in the road, pain would shoot through my body." At DeKalb we arranged for a suite with a bedroom, kitchen, bath and den, next to her room. Mama laughed and said, "That's the only cheap thing in the hospital."

She told us later how four or five different nurses had come in, asking her name, her doctor's name and why she was there. Mama said she kept thinking: *What is going on ? Can't they get this right?* She really chuckled when, after surgery, one of the nurses explained about all the questions.

"When the report came to us about your condition, we expected a cancer-ridden, dissipated little lady to come in. Then, you arrived."

One of the admitting nurses said, "I think there's been a mixup someplace. We didn't expect our patient to be in this good a condition."

"Well, I think we've got the wrong woman, too," another

agreed. "She's supposed to be 60 years old and that woman is not 60 years old."

A third nurse said, "I just don't believe it's the right woman."

Finally, after questioning Mama, the nurses met at their station and decided that, yes, they had the right woman. But they weren't going to do anything to Mama until they were sure.

Once settled in her room, Mama and I met Dr. Hartman, her surgeon. She loved to tell people, "He didn't fail in his bedside manner like some doctors do." Mama also liked his diplomatic candor. He told us that this was a bloody surgery and that there was a high percentage chance that she could be paralyzed in some way, if her heart made it through the operation.

As a top notch neurosurgeon, he already had three surgeries scheduled for Tuesday. He planned to do Mama between the second and third ones. Even as he talked to us, it was obvious that Mama, as the patient, was the one who would make the decisions.

We already knew Mama's heart might not survive six hours of surgery. Now, Dr. Hartman told us that he could make no promises. Until he got in there and saw the tumor, he didn't know what he was going to find. He explained that Mama could come out of the surgery with full paralysis. If that happened, machines would be required to keep her alive. It was possible that the time would come when none of her systems worked, and the machines would have to be turned off. He advised Mama to arrange for a living will and durable power of attorney to insure knowledge of her decisions, in the event that she was no longer able to make them for herself after surgery.

"This could be a six hour blood bath," Dr. Hartman continued. "And, if it is, the surgery will be very difficult around the spinal cord. If we come out of it clean, it's going to be a miracle of God." He then suggested to her, "Mrs. Williams, you need to think about what level of paralysis you could live with."

Mama quietly indicated to Dr. Hartman that no matter what paralysis resulted, she did not want to be placed on permanent life support.

We sat without speaking when the doctor left Mama's room.

It was a lot to digest, yet we appreciated his honesty. Then Mama said, "We don't know what the future holds. God knows that future, and you must understand that God may be very gracious and take me. If he does, I want you to recognize the fact that God has been gracious."

Before the Tuesday morning surgery, we took turns sitting beside Mama, telling her how much we loved her. Mama asked each of us in turn, "Is there anything that we need to get settled?" We cried together, laughed together, reminisced, and it was a marvelous experience. Finally, I told Mama, "You know, God has been so good to us. We've had time to say all the things we wanted to say to each other. We might not have to say good-bye right now, but we've had time to say good-bye. The Lord has been gracious to give us that opportunity."

Chapter Sixteen

Mama, the Miracle Lady

"WHAT A LOVELY DAY IT IS!" Mama said as she looked out the hospital window. The view from Mama's room consisted of rooftops and a parking garage. Nonetheless, Mama scanned the scenery as if she would never see it again. "Isn't God good?"

Dr. Hartman stopped by after his first surgery. Last night his job was to be the agent of reality. Now his role was that of a cheerleader.

He gave his pep talk and turned to leave the room. "I'll see you in surgery, about two o'clock."

"Dr. Hartman," Mama called after him. "Now about my dying."

He stopped dead in his tracks, shaking his head and rolling his eyes. He looked across at me as if to say, well, the pep talk didn't work this time.

Without looking at Mama, he declared, "We're not going to talk about dying today."

I reached over and patted his arm. *Hold the phone, Dr. Hartman,* I thought. *I've seen that sassy look in Mama before.*

"You see," Mama continued, "I'm being buried in a mausoleum and, well, the pink marble for the mausoleum hasn't gotten here from Italy. So I can't die today. There's no place to put me."

Laughing and shaking his head, Dr. Hartman breathed a sigh of relief. Mama winked back at the doctor. "It ain't over 'til the pink marble comes."

As we waited for her departure, many things were said as if it were the last time. Randy held her hand and, with deep-felt emotion, said, "You're the best mama any guy could have."

By phone, Tim assured her that he would never have made it without her belief in him.

I sat on the edge of the bed and she put an arm around me. "You've been more than a mama to me," I cried, "You've been my best friend. I always felt that you loved me no matter what I did. Even if you didn't like my actions, I knew you would always receive me with open arms. I fear that when you're gone I'll no longer have anyone to love me, no matter what. But because you've been here, I think I have the tools to survive." Our tears were flowing in unison. "Goodbye, Mama."

"Bye bye, my beautiful daughter." Reaching out, she stroked my face. "I'm so proud of you."

For years my parents had dealt with Dad's frequent departures by saying, "I'll see you in the morning." To them this meant, I'll see you when I get back from the trip. But if I don't make it back, I'll see you resurrection morning. "I'll see you in the morning," was also said as they drifted off to sleep.

I thought back to Mama's real rough periods when she first began battling the cancer. A country western song, *Love Me,* had meant a lot to her. It's the story of a young courting couple who were to meet, go to the nearest town, and get married. The bride was late and left a note for the groom that, in part, said, "If you get there before I do, don't give up on me." The song ends with the couple in their later years. The husband tells his wife as she is dying, "If you get there before I do, don't give up on me."

To Mama, this song framed her situation. She would get to heaven before Dad and he would be there in a little while.

As her gurney was pushed down the hall, all Dad could say was, "See you in the morning, darling."

The doctors did the surgery in a little over two hours—instead of six. When they came in to talk with us, Dr. Hartman and Dr. Feinberg were as excited as two little boys who had won a ballgame: There should be no paralysis.

"The surgery went great," Dr. Hartman reported, "and her heart showed only one little 'blip.' Apparently the radiation had shriveled the tumor so that its blood supply was gone. Without blood blocking our view, getting to the back of the spinal cord presented no problem. The tumor came out clean."

Dr. Hartman had removed the cancer-damaged vertebrae, and set a donor bone in Mama's neck. "We can't use glue, bolts or screws on the spine," Dr. Hartman continued. We should know in about six weeks if calcium is forming around the bone to make it adhere."

Over and over, I thought, *Thank you, Lord,* as the *Hallelujah Chorus* swirled inside my head.

When Mama was brought back to her room, she could hardly wait to tell us how Dr. Hartman had awakened her. "Well," he said, "it looks like the pink marble hasn't come yet."

"Miracle of miracles!" Dr. Hartman waltzed into Mama's room the next morning, saying, "You are our miracle lady! Normally, when I'm called in, the damage is already done and the patient is paralyzed. I don't often get to help somebody like this." He was still walking on air as he told Mama that her hospital recuperation period was to last several more days.

Being best friends with Mama sometimes came in real handy. Like, when I visited later that day. Mama was acting very strange. She was agitated and frustrated, very much unlike my mama. She wasn't normally a barker, but this day, I could have sworn she was a Doberman. I began to evaluate the situation and decided, since she had a friend visiting her at the time, to walk down and phone Mama from the pay phone.

"Mama," I said. "You seem very agitated to me."

"Yes, I am," she snapped.

"Now, Mama, I . . . I think—I'm not sure—but I think that the pain medication you're taking may be making you, uh, do some weird stuff. And it may also be making you feel so agitated."

Relief sounded in Mama's voice, as she said, "Well, my goodness! I'm glad somebody told me what was causing me to feel so weird. Now it all makes sense. I don't want to be in pain, but maybe it's time for me to move to Darvocet instead of this medicine. Maybe that would help me feel better."

After making the medication change, she told a friend, "My daughter called me and told me that I was losing it. But then I've often called my daughter and told her she was losing it."

Oftentimes, it is the daughter who does the caretaking of ill parents. But Randy stayed at the hospital the night after surgery and several days after Mama went home. I know it was not easy for him, but he did a terrific job in helping during those days. I really don't think I could have made it without him.

One of the days that Randy was sitting with Mama, a fellow came in with a stethoscope hanging around his neck. He kind of peeked around the corner, and Mama said, "Well, hello."

"Hello, Mrs. Williams," the gentleman responded. "How are you doing?"

"I seem to be doing fine."

"My colleagues have been keeping me informed about you. They tell me that you are a real miracle lady."

"Yes, it seems that way," Mama agreed.

"I just wanted to drop by and see how you were doing." He looked her in the eyes, as if he were trying to say more.

"Thank you," Mama responded graciously. The gentleman left shortly thereafter.

Randy, sitting in a chair by Mama, had observed this whole exchange. He said, "Who in the world was that man?"

Mama shrugged and said, "My son, that was the doctor I recently fired."

After we drew the line, all the professionals Mama worked with—except the doctor she fired—were very good, kind and gracious. We saw some excellent nurses, especially on the oncology floors. Not only were they sensitive, they were also interested in Mama as a person. They really cared about their patients.

One example of the nurses' wonderful insight occurred when Brittney came to visit. Brittney had been very upset about her grandmommie's surgery, so we decided that Brittney could come to Atlanta and spend the night at the hospital. We really didn't ask for approval, but the nurses knew of our plans and that it wasn't going to cause Mama any harm. And I was going to be there to make sure that all went well.

Brittney arrived, and I helped Mama move over to one side of the bed. Then Brittney got up on the bed and sat beside her. It seemed as if they sat for hours, talking about Brittney's school, her friends, and how Brittney was doing as a big sister. When I brought them some snacks, I overhead Mama telling her stories about when she was a little girl. Brittney was captivated. "Grandmommie," she kept saying, "Tell me one more story."

"Okay, honey," my mama replied. "This is the last one, because Grandmommie's awful tired." After Mama finished, they sat there watching TV and hugging each other. I really think they both needed that as part of their healing process.

Dr. Hartman had one more thing in mind. One of the disappointments Mama had faced as a result of having this surgery was that she would miss the big May 8th event at Luther Rice. The seminary was honoring her and Dad by naming the new administration building after them. Dad was moving from president to chancellor, and the school was giving him a reception. Dr. Hartman knew that this reception was real important to Mama, so he came in Friday morning and said, "Have you packed your bag yet? You are going to a reception today. I'm checking you out of the hospital. My only condition is that you walk into the reception. You can't ride—you can't be in a wheelchair—you've got to walk."

Mama wore a beautiful pink dress. Her makeup was fresh and she sported her best wig. And she was donning a huge neck collar. "It's not going to be easy," Mama said, "but I think I'll wear it as a badge of courage. This badge of courage is going to represent the courage of every single one of us."

Per Dr. Hartman's instructions, Mama walked into the reception. Luckily though, they had provided armchairs for Mama and Dad to sit in. As I looked at them, it occurred to me that that's how they had always been—side by side. Even when Dad was preaching on the other side of the world, they had been side by side. It was hard to know who was prouder of the other.

Many of the guests present came over to Mama to express praise to the Lord for her amazing recovery.

Margie McGiboney, a family friend and the one who catered this fabulous expression of love, came over to greet Mama. Mama looked at her and said, "Margie, you must have worked your fingers to the bone. It is a beautiful reception, but it means even more to me because I know that our good friend Margie put this all together."

Indeed, it was wonderful. There were tables filled with wonderful little morsels of food especially prepared for the grand occasion. Beautifully arranged flowers and candles adorned the linen covered tables. There wasn't a single thing missing at this event. Not even Miss Dottie was missing.

At three weeks post-op, Mama had her neck x-rayed to make sure the bones were still lined up right. Dr. Hartman nearly jumped for joy as he gave Mama the results. Calcium had already begun to form deposits around the donor bone—in half the expected time. Although she had to keep wearing the collar, Mama said that the little inconvenience was well worth the release from severe pain.

Mama enjoyed a beautiful relationship with her doctors. One day Dad accompanied her to an appointment with Dr. Lesser. The cardiologist joked and laughed with her, while still getting down to business.

With his examination over, he started to leave the room. Then he turned around, leaned over the exam table, and kissed Mama right on the cheek. Dad didn't know what to say.

When they got into the car Mama said, "Well, I guess you won't let me come out here by myself anymore."

"No, indeed!" By now, Mama and Dad were both laughing. "You won't come out here by yourself another time." They continued to chuckle. "My, my. Kissed on the cheek by a cardiologist," he teased.

It wasn't long after that Mama had another appointment with Dr. Lesser while Dad was out of town. Mama told me that the first thing Dad asked was, "Did you get your kiss?"

"Yes, indeed, I did. And I'm getting real spoiled."

Dad was in no way bothered by Dr. Lesser's kind affection toward Mama. I'm sure Dr. Lesser had no idea that, many times, those little kisses helped get her through.

Dr. Feinberg once told us, "A patient will spend days, weeks, months—if not years, researching the purchase of a home, a car or a major appliance. Yet, with his life, he'll go to only one doctor.When the doctor says, 'This is the diagnosis,' he'll accept it without question. And when the doctor says, 'This is it. Life is over,' the same patient accepts that as well. That's an incredible amount of trust to put in the hands of a single physician. Physicians are no different, no better than other people," Dr. Feinberg said. "We just happen to be trained in our field, just like a construction worker is trained to build a house."

Mama wanted a doctor that she could trust in full—one who was not afraid to declare war and fight the cancer. She felt that Dr. Feinberg thought as she did about her disease. They were partners in this crusade.

"Cancer patients are, by definition, people, too," Dr. Feinberg told our family. "It's very common for them to go through tremendous amounts of emotional stress. It's usually a sequence, beginning with denial: 'This can't be true. It can't be happening to me.' Then the anger sets in: 'This isn't fair,' they say. Next comes the fear stage: 'Oh, my God, this is real. This is true.' And, finally, depression: 'I guess this is it. There's nothing left to be done. No matter what happens, my life is over.' Unfortunately, many get trapped and can't go full circle. Those who cope and come through, then go through a process where they can be positive about their disease: 'This is the hand I've been dealt. I'll do all I can to make it the best that it can be.' It's a rare event to achieve that final stage."

Dr. Feinberg continued, "That's where Dorothy fits into what I call the empowerment phase: 'Well, this may be the best that I can be, but I'm not going to accept that. I'm going to make it even better still.' And they go one step beyond and start thinking in terms of 'what impact their lives can be: 'How can I do more? How can I affect positively the lives of other people with this disease?' "

Without question, he was talking about my mama. Mama's big, bad cancer became an opportunity to touch the lives around her. Countless times she would walk into the treatment room where other patients were receiving their chemotherapy. She'd sit in the recliner as they hooked her up to the chemo concoction of the day. Chatting with those around her, she began to develop relationships with those who were walking the same path. Frequently, Mama ministered to the angry patient, the fearful patient, or the defeated patient. "It seems to me," Mama would tell them, "we have two choices. We can either choose to lie down and just wait to be put in a coffin, or we can get out there in life and continue to live."

"If there is uniqueness with Dorothy," Dr. Feinberg said to us, "it's this: she succeeded in reaching the empowerment phase. There are only a few who ever reach that point of acceptance where they can give back to those around them who face the same crisis."

Spring returned, bringing new life and hope to 1993.

Over the years, Mama and Dad had talked about the house on a hill he wanted to build her. To Mama's delight, Dad found a cabin on a mountain near Hiawassee, Georgia, and rented it for the summer. It was three hours from Atlanta, and I was able to spend some long, lazy days with her. Dad was there between meetings.

The cabin almost formed a half moon, with a deck stretching across the back. Looking east, we could see the mountains of North Carolina framing a beautiful lake. Each evening's sunset seemed to outdo the one before. We had the best view on the whole mountain, and Mama loved the sweet smelling air.

Yet, even up here, Mama's appetite wasn't as good as before. In April, she got sick one Saturday night when Dad had to be away. I called her from Atlanta the next morning to tell her of my babysitting venture with Brittney and Ashlyn. Breaking in abruptly, she began telling me about her rough night. "Sandee," she moaned, "I'm so dehydrated. I had to crawl out to the refrigerator to get myself a drink. There I lay on the kitchen floor most of the night."

Knowing that Mama was alone, I listened as she continued to voice her distress. Finally, I said, "I'm coming up there. I'll load the girls in the car. Surely Joy and Tim will understand."

She shot back at me, "No. I don't want my grandchildren to see me like this."

I honored Mama's wish in spite of my desire to be with her.

By the next day Mama felt a little better and insisted that she would be okay until Dad returned in a few hours. A nagging thought darted across my mind. *Are we coming to the beginning of the end for Mama?*

During the summer Mama made several trips back and forth from her new Atlanta home to the cabin. In August she had a couple of sinking spells, as she described them. She felt exhausted and her heart would do weird things and beat irregularly. The doctors checked her blood sugar and ordered liver and kidney scans but found nothing to show that the cancer was growing. They gave her IVs with added potassium, changed some of her medicines, and sent her home. But, each time, it took longer for her to bounce back.

Later that month, my heart sank when Mama called me out of a counseling session. "I'm in trouble, Sandee. Please come."

When I got to the house, I found she had been in trouble for several hours and unable to get up. There was no mistaking her weakened condition.

I lifted her from the bed and changed her clothes and the bed linens. She had not eaten since breakfast, so I made her a light meal. I also called the cardiologist and spoke to his on-call nurse. She suggested we go to the hospital, but Mama was afraid to do that. Since she now looked more herself, I did not press the issue.

What I didn't know until much later was that she did not let Dad know how bad these "sinking spells" really were. She still feared he would stop preaching if he knew.

Fall came on and Mama rallied a bit. "You know, I'd really like to see London again," she mused one day. "Do you suppose we could go for Thanksgiving this year?"

Dad and I agreed to take her and she began planning our trip. Her eyes sparkled every time we discussed it. But then, while Dad was away again, she had to call me to come help her a couple of times during the night. Again, she resisted going into the hospital because "my diabetes will get messed up there." So, her doctors helped her get things under control at home.

Finally, one week before we were to leave, Mama conceded, "I just cannot make the trip to London. Sandee, you go on and enjoy the trip. Take your friend, Melanie Carstarphen, and have a good time."

A few days before we were to leave, I called to talk to Mama. Dad answered the phone and relayed that Mama didn't feel like talking. I said, "Put her on the phone, please." And he did.

"Mama, don't do that to me. The last time I called your dad and mother, your dad didn't feel like talking, so we didn't. A few days later he was dead. Don't do that to me. Let us have the opportunity to talk—even if it's just to hear each other breathe."

Mama came back with, "You're right." And she didn't do that to me again. While there was still time, I didn't want to miss any opportunity to talk. After all, she was my best friend.

The Sunday before my trip, I felt impressed to check on a few things before leaving the country. I ran by the funeral home to see if a cherry casket was available. And it was. I stood in the teal and pink foyer of the funeral home. It looked as if Mama had decorated it herself with lovely Queen Anne furniture. *Yeah, this looks like Mama's kind of place, I thought.*

On my way out the door, I grabbed one of their business cards, still hoping I would not have to use it.

I jumped back into my white Blazer and headed toward Interstate 20. From the highway, I again saw the gracious, southern, Colonial-style mausoleum. As I guided the Blazer through the lawn of the cemetery, I thought, *I wonder if the pink marble's in yet*? I went inside, and there it was.

The day Melanie and I were to leave, we ran over to see Mama before catching our flight. While Melanie visited with Mama, I made a few phone calls. Melanie told me later that she and Mama hugged, then Melanie said, "You make sure you're here when we get back. Don't you leave until Sandee gets back."

In a thin, weak voice, Mama replied, "I'll try."

Melanie and I went to London and did exactly what Mama instructed: "Have a terrific time."

Tim and Joy came after Thanksgiving to visit Mama and

Dad. They told me later how concerned they were with her appearance. For the first time, Mama didn't let Brittney spend the night because "I'm just too tired." She still resisted going back into the hospital because she felt she could control her food intake and sugars better herself. Again, she didn't tell Dad how bad she was, for fear he'd cancel his meetings.

As Melanie and I were flying back from London, I told my friend, "When I get home, I'm going to have to deal with some kind of tragedy. I don't know what it is, but I sense that something bad is going to happen."

Melanie looked at me as if I had read her mind. "I've felt the same way, Sandee."

Melanie and I arrived on Tuesday. I drove over to see Mama that night. She was so excited as I told her all about the trip. "Oh, I'm so glad y'all had such a good time," she repeated several times, enjoying it vicariously.

"But, Mama, how are you feeling?"

"Dr. Lesser had me go for some heart tests this morning. I don't have the results back." She didn't seem overly concerned. Then, Mama said, "Honey, I'm very tired. You must be, too, so why don't you just go on home." Such a suggestion was uncommon for Mama.

Wednesday afternoon, Dr. Lesser called Mama. "It looks like you have had some silent heart attacks and there's been considerable damage. I don't want you to move around much. I want you to be very still." Mama agreed, as Dad waited attentively for her to repeat the test results.

Later that night, Dad called me. "You know, she's really not doing well."

"Dad, if you're that concerned, take her to the hospital."

"She won't go to the hospital."

"Well, there's a time when you have to take her anyway." His sigh told me he was torn between doing what needed to be done and pleasing Mama.

Fifteen minutes later my phone rang again. This time Dad sounded panicked. "Sandee, she has collapsed on the floor and I can't get her up. I've called 911." As we talked, the EMTs rushed into the room and began preparing Mama for another ambulance ride.

"We're walking out the door," Dad told me. "We are going to DeKalb, where your mother had her last surgery. I can't talk anymore."

"I'll meet you there, Dad." My insides felt as empty as the phone sounded after Dad hung up.

At DeKalb I found Dad sitting in a secluded little room where they put you when they think your loved one is about to die. Dad was silently crying. My tears joined his.

A few minutes later, the hospital advocate peeked in the door. "You can go in now to see Mrs. Williams."

Mama was alert and talking, but her pulse was weak and thready. She asked for her slippers and I got them for her. Just as the nurses began to ask about her medical history, I saw Mama's heart flatline on the monitor. The doctor calmly turned and said, "Y'all need to leave." As the hospital advocate ushered us out, we heard the doctors and nurses pulling up their equipment to defibrillate her heart.

Again, Dad and I waited in the little room for news.

Once Mama's heart was beating again, she was moved to the Coronary Critical Care Unit, with a temporary pacemaker in place. Her kidneys had shut down enough that her body wasn't clearing its excess potassium. Jaundice made the whites of her eyes look as if they had egg yolk on them.

Aware of her critical condition, the nurses let Dad and me stay at Mama's bedside as much as we wanted until we left around three-thirty Thursday morning.

In the meantime, I phoned Randy and Tim. They arranged flights to get them to Atlanta at seven thirty a.m. Jim Kennebrew, a friend who taught at Luther Rice, met Randy and Tim and immediately drove them to the hospital where they met Dad.

As I drove back to the hospital from my house, I called the CCU waiting room over my cellular phone. Jim Kennebrew answered. "She isn't doing well, Sandee. You need to hurry."

Dread enveloped me. "Tell her not to leave until I get there."

In the days after Mama's original cancer diagnosis, we made promises to each other. Mama promised me that she would not quit fighting until I said it was okay. I promised her plain truth when the fight became hopeless.

When I arrived back at the hospital, Mama could no longer talk. However, her eyes were open and she clearly indicated that she understood what was said to her. When Mama heard my voice, she started thrashing around, trying to see me. I knew she wanted me to keep my promise and tell her honestly where she was. I walked out to the nurses station. "Can you please get Dr. Feinberg on the phone for me?"

Once he answered, I asked, "How viable is our situation?"

"It isn't. She will not make it through this day."

Dad and the boys had gone to complete admission information when I returned to Mama's room. She turned her head and looked at me square in the eyes. Her expression said, "Now, tell me the truth."

"Mama, I talked with Dr. Feinberg. He said that your heart is not going to hold up, and you need to know that. He said there's not much chance that you'll be able to hold on very long."

Mama looked at me like, "Well, I needed to know that." She grew very calm. After that, she drifted in and out of awareness. But Dad, Randy, Tim and I were able to say many of the things on our hearts during her periods of lucidness. We said a lot of our goodbyes, realizing that she probably wouldn't be with us much longer.

During one of my talks, I was able to tell her, "Really, Mama, I'm going to be okay. I'm going to make it." I wanted her to know she didn't have to worry about me.

Friends begin gathering in the waiting room, until there were fifty or more. They, too, were allowed time at her bedside. I now admitted to myself that in human terms, there was no way Mama was going to make it though the day. I gave the attending nurse the card with the funeral home's name and number but continued to pray that we wouldn't have to use it—yet.

That night Mama began to rally. The nurses kept expressing utter amazement that this was happening. As she began coming around, Mama said, "Get my purse over there." After a few minutes, she said, "I need to get in one of my bags." But we had none of those things there.

"Mama, look at me," I asked. "Where are you?"

Indeed, she looked at me, as if to say, "You fool." Then, irritated, she said, "I'm in the hospital. DeKalb Hospital."

"Then you know that we don't have any of your things here."

She thought for a moment, then said, "Well, then, go get my things."

Dr. Feinberg commented that he knew she was doing better when she started giving orders.

Randy and Tim decided they would stay the night with her. Randy took the first shift and Tim the second. When Dad and I returned, they reported she'd had a difficult night, with the high levels of potassium still not under control.

On Friday, she was even more alert and talkative. Much of Thursday was a fog to her, but she did remember hearing Dad say, "Hang on, Dorothy. Don't quit, just hang on."

She could recount for us just what had happened in the ER during the time she flatlined, though. Mama said, "I was awake through the whole thing." Again, the nurses and doctors were amazed. There hadn't been enough blood and oxygen going to her brain to explain her memory or ability to function at this level. "She's our miracle lady," the nurses and doctors repeated.

That night, the three or four empty beds in Critical Care filled up. When they needed more space, the staff talked to me about transferring Mama to the Telemetry Unit. Dr. Feinberg told me, "They need the bed. If Dorothy needed to be here right now, I'd have her stay. But she is rallying, and she would not want to keep someone else from being cared for." I knew that was true. So, she was moved without question.

Dr. Feinberg then told us it was his weekend off. "Here's the name of the doctor who will be covering for me."

Feeling that Mama had turned another miraculous corner, Randy flew back to Tampa. Tim flew home to Jacksonville for a few hours, only to return to Atlanta for a revival in Rutledge, Georgia. He planned to stop by to see Mama after each evening's meeting.

Dad and Mama had all day Saturday together.

Sunday morning, Dad called me. "Sandee, I'm on my way back in. Your mother called and said she's sick."

I drove back to the hospital and found Mama hot and sweating profusely. She didn't have a fever—in fact her temperature was only ninety-five degrees. Then she started getting cold and her temperature dropped to ninety-one. The staff warned us that it was not going to be very long now, because her heart was very bad.

She got colder and colder. About three o'clock that Sunday afternoon, her nurse gave Mama 200 milligrams of Darvocet to cover her pain. The jaundice which had gone away began to return as her kidneys shut down again.

Mama was pleased when told that Sandy Kennebrew, her nurse, the wife of Jim Kennebrew, planned to sit with her that night.

As Mama's condition continued to deteriorate, Dad began to ask what else could be done for her. "What about giving her some Lasix so she won't build up fluid?

Sandy explained that since Mama's heart was not beating well, the Lasix would only cause other body systems to malfunction. And that might cause her to be in pain.

"What about another temporary pacemaker?" Dad asked. "It helped before."

"Yes," came the response, "but that was to get her over the cardiogenic shock. That's no longer a problem. The pacemaker only regulates the heart's beat but cannot make it stronger."

It was then that the cardiologist told us about the IV Dopamine Mama had received. It usually gives the patient twenty-four to forty-eight hours. We can't possibly give her IV Dopamine continuously."

We thought Mama had turned another corner when she improved again and that maybe we could find out what was causing her sinking spells. Suddenly it was clear that the Dopamine had allowed her to rally. Tears filled my eyes as I realized it probably had given her all the time she was going to get. But we'd had four beautiful days. During three of these she'd been alert and her old spunky self.

I had to run home to deal with a plumbing emergency. The plumber finished at eleven p.m., just in time for a call from Sandy Kennebrew. "Her heart rate's getting a little bit low. You'd better come on back to the hospital, Sandee."

When I arrived, the nurse was giving Mama atropine, a medicine to speed the heart up. She gave it every five minutes through Mama's IV, hoping to allow time for Tim to arrive before Mama lost consciousness. I sat on Mama's bed and pulled her arms around me. Mama looked at me with a puzzled expression. "What are you doing?" she said.

"I just wanted to feel your arms around me one more time."

She smiled and said, "I'll try." Moments later, Mama shook her head and said, "I don't want to die. I want to do what God wants, but I don't want to die." Yet, there was no panic in her voice or face. And she indicated she was absolutely pain-free. Mama's being pain-free appeared to be a gift from God, because she hadn't had any pain medication since mid-afternoon.

Tim slipped in a few minutes later. Mama and Tim talked about how they loved each other. Mama said to Tim, "I am very proud of you."

We located Randy on the phone and he and Mama talked for a few minutes. Mama closed with, "You're wonderful and I love you."

As the nurse stopped giving the atropine, Mama looked at Dad. "I would like to see what God is going to do with my grandchildren."

By this time, Mama's heart was beating only twenty times a minute, and the nurses could not believe she was still alert. With so little oxygen going to Mama's brain, she should have been comatose. Again God's blessings were evident.

Seeing that Dad and Tim were busy handling their own separation anxiety, I began to wonder if I could make it through what I knew was going to happen. I called my friend Margie McGiboney. She and her husband, Chuck, came to support me.

Soon after that, Mama slipped into what Dad called a deep

sleep, but I guess it was a coma. The nurses indicated that we should not expect her to make it another twenty minutes. She was in a dying heart pattern, and her heart rate was so bad.

We continued to hold Mama's hand and caress her. I began to sing, "What a fellowship, what a joy divine . . .." Tears streamed down my face. "Leaning on the everlasting arms . . .." By now, I could barely see Mama through my tears, but I continued. "I have blessed peace with my Lord divine . . .."

I knew at that moment, there was no hope of Mama's staying with us. I wanted to proclaim that she needed to be leaning on the everlasting arms.

When I began to sing the chorus, I was not surprised that Dad and Tim joined me. To my amazement, the nurses on duty began to sing as well. We sang such songs as,'*Tis So Sweet To Trust In Jesus*, and *What A Friend We Have In Jesus*.

As though she were singing right along with us, Mama raised her eyebrows and leaned her head back when we hit the high notes. We were bound and determined to hold her, caress her and sing her all the way into gloryland.

When Mama continued to hang on, the nurses asked me, "Is there any unfinished business she has to take care of?"

"No."

"Is she waiting for a child or somebody close to come?"

"No."

"Well, why is she still hanging on?"

"You have to keep in mind, this is a woman who beat the odds when they said she only had three months to live. This is the woman who fought to live through congestive heart failure, various surgeries, chemo and radiation, and finally, spinal surgery. This is the woman who lived when everyone said she would not, and she's still fighting to live."

Dad's role had been that of Mama's cheerleader. Now, needing to encourage her until she could no longer go on, he told her, "Breathe, Dorothy, breathe." Then he would tell her how beautiful she was, inside and out.

The Christian nurses on duty that night came in and prayed with us. One of them told us, "I hate working on Sunday, because I miss church. But, I've been on holy ground tonight. It is clear that the presence of the Lord has been here. This has been a holy place." Again, they called Mama a miracle woman because she continued to live while in the dying heart pattern.

Around two o'clock Monday morning, one of the nurses working with Mama led the man in the next room to a saving knowledge of the Lord Jesus. We could sense the power of God and the presence of angels.

I had never seen a person die, and I hated to see my mama die. But, at the same time, it was a blessing to be there. Mama exhibited peace, but it was still a struggle for her to breathe. There might be almost a minute between breaths. I would think, *oh, she's gone*. Then, suddenly she would breathe again. She kept hanging in there. It wasn't that she was so strong physically, but our miracle woman wanted to live.

I learned later that around five o'clock that morning, Mama's monitor showed her heart starting to pick up a little bit. It became more regular. The nurses said they just looked at each other in awe. They had already seen things that were beyond medical explanation.

Dad had stayed in her room all night. I reflected on all the times Mama, in her cancer state, had sent him to preach in the face of other Christians' condemnation. To her amazement, Christian brothers and sisters thought he should have left the ministry to care for her. She respected God's anointing on Dad and did not want her cancer to keep anyone from having a personal relationship with Christ.

God honored her sacrifice and allowed Dad to be home at all the times when Mama really needed him. Dad was the one who drove her to radiation each day back at the beginning. Over the last three years, they spent every available minute together. Now Dad was at her side, loving and caring for her as no one else could.

Over and over, Dad told Mama how much he loved her and what a wonderful wife she had been to him. Tim and I again told her how much she meant to us. We continued to love her and praise the Lord.

About six o'clock, I lay down for about fifteen minutes on the fold-out bed in the room. When I got up, Tim rested for another fifteen minutes. It was after this that we began to release Mama and give her permission to die, if necessary.

Finally, about seven thirty, Dad went to the restroom. Tim had stepped out, too. Finding myself alone with Mama, I leaned over and kissed her cheek. "Mama, I think it's time for you to go. I don't want you to go, but if you have to, it's all right." Then I caressed her forehead and said, "Mama, the pink marble has come in."

Dad slipped back into the room. He, too, seemed to begin to release Mama as he said, "I don't want you to leave, Dorothy. But I know you may have to go on." Up to now Dad had continued to pray for a miracle of healing. This time, he prayed, "God, I believe that You have the power needed to heal Dottie, and I don't want You to take her. But, Lord, we understand if You have to take her."

About fifteen minutes later, she was breathing so hard that when she took her last breath it was clear that life on earth was over. "Well," Dad said, "I guess the pink marble has arrived."

Just then, Dr. Feinberg came onto the floor. He had been paged and didn't understand why. Mama was doing so well when he left on Friday that he planned to dismiss her later that morning. He, too, expressed disbelief as he examined the monitor strips showing the dying heart pattern for almost nine hours.

Brenda, one of the nurses, summed up Mama's homegoing this way. "You do not die any better than you live. To die as beautifully and as sweetly as Dorothy Williams, walking with the Lord in the dark hours like that, she had to have had a life that was dynamic."

Chapter Seventeen

The Celebration of Mama

MAMA HAD LIVED THREE YEARS AND THREE DAYS since her cancer was diagnosed. During that time, she had told us more than once: "I don't want my funeral to be a sad affair but a celebration of my homegoing. There should be lots of singing—songs like *What A Friend We Have In Jesus* and *'Tis So Sweet To Trust In Jesus*. I'd like Dr. Homer Lindsay to preach the service. Then, I want the Rogers—Ben and Nita—and Shirley Lindsay to share in the eulogy. But they are to brag on God and not on me."

"That sounds fine, Mama," we had agreed.

"There won't be many at my service," Mama had predicted. "Nobody here in Atlanta knows me."

Now, as God's protective numbness enveloped our family, Tim placed calls to the Lindsays and Rogers, telling them Mama's fight was finally over. We began arranging the service according to Mama's instructions.

Friends brought food. Randy, Christa, Reagan, and Judson arrived. Mechanically, I took Mama's clothes to the funeral home. I knew that just beyond my present numbness lay an emptiness I did not want to face.

When I awoke the morning of the service, my thoughts overwhelmed me. *I can't do this. I can't make it through the funeral.* I showered and dressed, still repeating, "I'm not going to make it." Finally, still unsure that I could hold together through the service, I joined Dad and the others.

As our family was ushered into the chapel, I saw that its pews were filled. *And Mama thought no one would be here,* I remembered. Usually right, this time Mama really underestimated the lives she had touched. Nearly 200 people—including many preachers from other states—had come to pay their respects. Then, seated beside Dad, I heard Dr. Jerry Vines greet the congregation as the service began: "The family wants this service to be a celebration, as we rejoice in the homegoing of Dottie Williams." I felt the peace of God surround me.

Dr. Richard Lee, Mama's Atlanta pastor, offered the opening prayer and read Scripture. Nodding to us, he said, "I want to thank the family for letting me know Dottie Williams. Last Saturday afternoon, I visited her hospital room. She looked at me and simply said, "I want the last moments I have in my life to tell for Jesus, and be a witness to somebody.' And it was, and it is now."

"Rejoice," the Luther Rice ladies' trio, sang *Hallelujah, Praise the Lord*. Following that, the congregation joined in one stanza each of, *'Tis So Sweet To Trust In Jesus, Leaning On The Everlasting Arms,* and *What A Friend We Have In Jesus*.

The songs were glorious. At times, laughter filled the chapel—especially when Ben Rogers reminded us of God's hand in bringing together the little ole' redheaded girl and the handsome young preacher. "I'd rather hear Dorothy Williams laugh than hear anybody sing or preach. She could just lift you up with that laugh. But she had to have it, because she had a big burden to bear for the Lord." Then, Ben spoke to Randy, Tim, and me. "No one could have had a better mother. She loved each one of you in a unique way. Don't ever forget the touch of Mama and the blessing of her life." Ben's eyes held on Dad's. "And to my brother, Gene. We love you and pray for you."

"Dottie became the sister I never had," Nita Rogers said. "Both of us were called to be preachers' wives before we were twenty. We had wonderful children to talk about and super grandchildren. We shared giggles, work, rest, and travel together. Dottie was the personification of the Proverbs 31 woman."

Shirley Lindsay spoke of Mama as her friend. "I was introduced to Dottie, and something clicked. That was the Holy Spirit bringing us together. When Dottie entered a room, that room was filled with love and laughter and fun.

"She was a woman who led other women to want to know

the Lord as Saviour, and to live, in Jesus Christ, a holy life. I thank God for the fragrance of a dear, godly lady, my friend, Dottie."

Betty Hall, Dad's secretary for eleven years, also called Mama "a dear friend," and told of Mama's commitment to getting the Lord's work done. "Dottie wanted everything in order everywhere, so souls could be saved.

"I've never known a woman who had more faith in the Lord, more courage, and belief that He was truly in control of her life. She never complained but accepted every day as the Lord gave it to her. Not only in her illness, but for as long as I have known her.

"Dottie did everything that was necessary so Dr. Williams would be ready to go out and preach the Word. And, because she did it so well, I'm sure there are many things that Dr. Williams still is not aware of.

"For instance, when she was so sick one day recently, I went by the house to see about her. She was standing in the kitchen, trying to make soup. She'd scrape a carrot, and go lie down. She'd scrape a carrot and go lie down. Then, she'd try to peel a potato.

"Finally I said, 'Dottie, let me do it for you.'

"'No,' she said. 'Gene needs the strength from homemade soup. He loves homemade soup and I want to do this for him. He's coming home tomorrow.' I've never known a wife more dedicated to being a servant in the Lord's work."

Dr. Homer Lindsay spoke for all of us as he began his sermon. "Dottie preached her service by the life she lived. That's the way all of us ought to be living."

Then, reading from the Bible: "'So when this corruptible shall have put on incorruption' (1 Corinthians 15:54)—you know, I couldn't help think about Dottie, 'cause her body did stay with her spirit and her heart. She had so many problems—sugar diabetes, the heart problem, and the long siege with cancer. The corruptible has now been done away, and she has put on the incorruptible.

"'And this mortal shall have put on immortality, then shall be brought to pass the saying that is written, Death is swallowed up in victory. O, death, where is thy sting. O, grave, where is thy victory? (1 Cor. 15:54-55)

"Now, this is true for Dottie, it has been swallowed up in victory. This is not true for y'all. There is a sting, there is a hurt. You can't escape it. Gene, you're going to be helpless. You're going to have to learn to do everything—learn how the vacuum cleaner operates and how the washing machine operates, how to keep from burning water, and all that.

"For you children, it's tough to lose your mother. You don't get over that. You just don't get over it. By having such a loving, sweet, and gracious mother as you had, it's going to make it even harder.

"'But thanks be to God, which giveth us the victory through our Lord Jesus Christ. Therefore, my beloved brethren, be ye steadfast, unmoveable, always abounding in the work of the Lord, forasmuch as ye know that your labor is not in vain in the Lord.' (1 Corinthians 15:57-58)

"This casket is empty. It just holds the remains that she lived in. This, you know, is the heart of Christianity. This is the heart of all of it. The resurrection power. She's with the Lord. She's a spirit; she doesn't have that body yet, but she will. All of us will one day. It's going to be great. What a reunion. But we gotta be busy now. Keep on winning souls. Keep on making soul-winning your priority. That's what heaven cares about. Heaven cares about getting souls saved."

Dr. Lindsay focused on my brothers and me. "Your mother did a good job. Be faithful to her, her memory, and Jesus. Keep on the soul-winning track. Getting people saved is what it's all about."

God's peace descended on me as I realized again how Mama had allowed God to use her life. She trusted Him, so I knew I could, too.

After the service, friend after friend and former students spoke of Mama's faith and kindness to them. A bank vice-president said: "I'd never been to a funeral that wasn't sad. I actually left there happier than when I went in. It was a joyful time."

We knew we had celebrated Mama's homegoing her way.

From the time of the funeral, I stored a reservoir of tears and pain. I had kept myself busy doing tasks expected of a first child. I was putting things in order. As I went about accomplishing my daughterly duties, I stopped feeling.

I remember hearing someone on the phone saying coldly, "Sandee, all you need to do is just go on with your life. Besides, your mother wouldn't be too happy with you if she could see how sad you are now."

I quietly thought, *it's just been six weeks and I felt I was dealing with the loss okay . . . at least in public*.

"If you are a Christian, you should not have difficulty with your mother's death," this friend continued. "After all, she is in heaven and you should be rejoicing. I don't believe your mother would be pleased if you're too sad. Grief does not honor her."

I don't remember much after that except I ended the conversation rather quickly because I could no longer hold back the flood of tears.

Sitting in Mama's rocking chair, I began to come to myself. I felt a cold dampness on my face. I tried to focus on what it was that was touching me, but it was dark. I couldn't see. *When had it become dark? It was just lunchtime*, I thought. I tasted the salt of tears. As I reached to wipe my face, I felt my new little poodle beat me to it. Spankee, my little buddy, was licking the tears from my face. My eyes finally focused as the black puppy cocked his head and looked at me, as if to say, "What in the world is the matter with you?" I realized at that moment I had lost part of the day.

Without meaning to do so, this friend had propelled me down the road of grief. Although the path was gut-wrenching, it was a path I had to walk. As I realized what had happened that afternoon, I knew I was now missing Mama.

I no longer felt that she was just out of town. My heart experienced what my head already knew, which was that in earthly terms, I would never hear her speak again, or see her face. The finality pierced the depth of my soul. The pain was almost unbearable, even to the point of feeling an intense pressure in my chest. It was as if someone had reached into my body and ripped out a part of my heart.

At times, thoughts battled inside my head until I was utterly confused. I loved Mama and didn't want her to suffer any longer. Likewise, I wanted to rejoice in her heavenward graduation. But she was gone forever from my life. I knew and believed that she had a life in Christ, and that indeed comforted me in a spiritual sense. But it did not diminish the physical and emotional pain that ravaged my very being.

My love for her became a perplexing question. Did I love her for her sake, or did I love her for mine? The answer to this dilemma did indeed create the basis for my recovery. Did I want her to remain on earth because I did not want to feel the loss, or did I want her to go forward through death because it was indeed best for her? All I knew was that the abyss of my loss and pain was balanced by the depth of my love for her.

Although Mama's homegoing was a holy and glorious experience, the memory that penetrated my mind was that one moment she was here and the next moment she was not. Everything changed in that one moment. Nothing was safe for me, her child, anymore. Nothing would ever be the same. But, then, that was how it was supposed to be.

At the funeral, people had come to me and said, "Oh, you're handling things so beautifully, Sandee." I couldn't understand this, because I was a zombie. All I wanted to do was crawl into a corner and cry.

In the days following, some of the Christian folks I knew said such things as:

"Your mother's out of her misery, and you should be joyful that she is in a better place."

"Just remember, all things work together . . .."

"You know that God won't put on you any more than you can handle."

Those were Christian cliches that I expected to hear. I did not for one moment doubt the truth of what these friends said, but they did not make the pain go away. What I was unprepared to hear was, "Sandee, you knew that she was going to die, so you should have been better prepared." But the most hurtful thing that I heard was, "So-and-so handled this better than you are handling it."

I knew these people had good intentions. Nonetheless, I wanted to slap them because their words discounted my hurt and grief. This created in me the desire to validate my hurt all the more. It was as if they were directly or indirectly saying that my profession as a counselor should eliminate the need for grief. My professional ability and my Christianity were being questioned because I actually grieved. Maybe they wanted to eliminate my grief because it was outside their comfort zones. This, of course, had nothing to do with whether grief was good for me. Maybe they thought by giving me sympathy they were giving me permission to grieve. Or possibly there was a fear inside of them that if they talked to me, they might feel the need to "fix it." But it couldn't be fixed.

All I wanted to do was to talk about my hurt because, by not talking about it, the pain became more intense. And what I needed most was someone to just listen. I asked myself, "What do you do with a person in grief?" My answer was simply, "Nothing; just be there."

Words from Mama echoed through my mind: "Life is a process of learning and growing. God never promised that this process would be pain-free. But remember, my darling daughter, the goodness that comes from any of this is that you have an opportunity . . . an opportunity to become more like Christ." So, I began to ask myself an important question, "What is grief?"

What I came to was that grief is a normal response to loss, and it is a road we all must walk. But I noted that everyone walked this road differently. Grief for me was a process which included denial, anger, physical and emotional anguish, and a hope for future acceptance. I knew if I missed any aspect of this process, I might rumble around in my misery for many years to come. And, if I was Mama's daughter, I would take each step of grief with great gusto.

Grief also was exampled to me by Christ. Besides the fact that Scripture tells us that Jesus was in obvious anguish over the death of his dear friend Lazarus, I personally began to see my Lord's time in the Garden of Gethsemane to include grief.

Jesus entered the garden just hours before he was to be crucified. He left His disciples with instructions to pray. The Word said that He withdrew from them about a stone's throw away, and began himself to pray.

"Father, if thou be willing, remove this cup from me; nevertheless, not my will, but thine, be done. And there appeared an angel unto him from heaven, strengthening him. And being in an agony, he prayed more earnestly; and his sweat was, as it were, great drops of blood falling down to the ground." (Luke 22:42-44.)

Christ knew that He was to experience death, and He knew that the sins of the world would be placed upon Him. He would not become a sinner, but He would become sin for us. It was likewise obvious that on the cross He would be separated from the earthly family He had known. If my Lord was in such agony as to sweat, "as it were, great drops of blood" because of the events ahead, then why should the chasm of my grief be discounted?

If the grief of my Lord Jesus Christ was honorable, then why would my grief over the death of Mama not be honorable as well? Mama's union with Christ was a proof of the perfection of His love. And her willingness to trust in Him would be proven when she met Jesus "face to face."

My mama was in gloryland. She was home. My mind tried to envision her in her new surroundings. I tried to think of what she would be doing at this time. I began to chuckle. Mama had given all of her singing talent to me, and she was left with virtually none. But, I knew that today, she was a terrific chorister in the heavenly choir.

I thought of the frequent times Mama and Dad had moved from place to place. She always laughed in amazement that Dad somehow had a revival scheduled on moving day. This never bothered her because she forged ahead to put things in place and to light the home fires.

I knew this to be true, even in her death. Mama had gone

before Dad one more time to light the home fires and prepare for his coming to join her. Upon his arrival, a place will be set for him, and they will forever light the home fires together.

Finally I reflected on a time during the early days of Mama's fight to live. I was visiting Randy in Tampa. My little brother, methodical as always, began to summarize what he viewed as Mama's perception of her purpose as "a mother." "You know, Sandee," Randy said. "Mama was always clear about her calling to motherhood. It was obvious she had purposed in her heart to teach us how to live. I remember hearing her say that a mother's children are only on loan from God. And that the toughest job for a mother was to teach them how to leave the nest and stand on their own."

"Yeah, Randy, Mama never was very clingy. I guess that's why it was so pleasant to be around her. She didn't enmesh herself in our lives, and she had a healthy balance of detachment which gave us the space to stand on our own. Because she didn't demand any 'royal appearances,' she made me want to be with her all the more. Yep, she saw motherhood as synonymous with teacher."

"Mama diligently taught us how to live," Randy continued. "She even booted us out of the nest because she wanted us to learn how to live without her. A mother, she believed, only became successful when her children became self-sustaining. We'll soon know what it's like to live without her. And Mama has given us the tools to do so. Sandee, Mama has taught us how to live, and now—just as she promised—she is teaching how to die."

P. S.

My Letters to Mama

12/12/93
Dear Mama,

It's been almost a week now, and Dad is having a real hard time. He particularly is having difficulty seeing your personal things hanging in the closets, filling the dresser and lying on the bathroom vanity. Because you always said that you never wanted anyone to die and go to hell because of you, Dad decided to keep his preaching commitment today. He asked me if I could somehow get your things moved while he was away. This afternoon Ruth Flanagan and Steve and Vivian Cox helped me by packing everything in boxes and moving it to my garage. I know it seems a bit soon to do this, but Dad is hurting so. Maybe, I can go through them later when I feel more up to it.

While I was at your house, I found two unsigned sympathy cards on your desk. At first I was confused. Mama, you don't usually send sympathy cards, and I don't know anyone in our lives who has died except you. After reading them, it finally dawned on me. You had gotten these cards for me and Dad. One of the cards said, "Meet God in the morning and go with Him through the day . . . You will never in your lifetime face another hopeless day." The other card again spoke to my heart, "When God's ready and waiting to share the burden you find too heavy to bear . . . Let go and let God lead the way." Somehow, you knew we would need to hear from you such an affirmation. Your wisdom was great because it came from God.

Thanks, Mama,
Sandee

12/24/93
Dear Mama,

Well, we survived Christmas Eve. We had all our usual foods and under the tree were a ton of gifts. It was very strange for you not to be there. What was somewhat of a unique blessing was to receive the last Christmas present from you. In spite of the fact you had been sick unto death, you had made sure each of us had an expression of your love, a Christmas gift. We all took our turn at crying.

Earlier today I found a picture of you and Dad at our first cancer Christmas. You didn't want the wheelchair in this picture so you stood on your right leg. I'm glad we made that picture and I'm glad we had that time together.

Love,
Sandee

1/17/94

Dear Mama,

I was going through some of your papers today and guess what I found? I ran across a letter dated June 14, 1948, written from you to Mammaw Miller. This was just about two weeks before your wedding.

If you were here, you would laugh. You discussed all kinds of preparations for the wedding such as the ushers, the flowers and the rehearsal dinner. In the midst of all this, you very innocently wrote, "Your letter was very sweet. It has meant so much to me. You are one of the sweetest and nicest people I know. Gene just couldn't have had a more wonderful mother than you." Can you believe that? And just think, it was only two weeks later that you were taking your walk to reconsider your decision to marry.

Along with the letter, I found some pictures. One was of just Mammaw Miller. The other two were of her and Henry, in a rather dapper hat, and her and Sam in front of their house.

I wonder if you had really known what was ahead of you when you wrote that letter, would you have gone on with it? I suspect you would have. You were always a gutsy lady. Besides, I know of your love for Dad.

Proud of you,
Sandee

1/30/94

Dear Mama,

I desperately missed you this afternoon. I always looked forward to our Sunday afternoons together. But today was particularly hard. Early this afternoon I threw some of your dirty clothes into the washer. After they were dry, I began to fold them as I was watching a good ol' black-and-white movie on TV. I was making good progress when I pulled out the pink gown you were wearing when you went to the hospital for the last time. I was really concentrating on the movie as I felt for the seams of the gown in order to finish folding it. But, I couldn't find the seams. I looked away from the movie and at the gown. My heart stopped as I gasped. The gown had been cut right down the middle. Bless your heart, they had cut the gown off you in the emergency room.

My heart hurts. I miss you so much. Because you are not here, there is a silence. There has never been such a silence.

But I made it through the day. I just kept looking at three sets of pictures of you and Dad. You know the one of ya'll in your twenties, and then in your forties, and finally in your sixties. Those faces reminded me of the wonderful times we had through all those years.

Missing you,
Sandee

2/14/94
Dear Mama,

The best valentines for me today were the cards you and Dad gave each other last year. Dad's card was filled with pink roses and a lovely message. But the message that touched me was the one he wrote. I remember he cried when he gave it to you.

"You are the most precious person in my life," he wrote. "You have always been beautiful, sweet, cheerful and loving. You are smart, comfortable, sexy and you have produced and raised three of the finest children a couple could ever have. I have been the most blessed man I know, because I have the greatest wife a man ever had. My Lord gave me His second greatest gift when He gave you to me. I love you more **now** *than ever."*

The message of the card you gave Dad was, "Let's be wild! Let's be crazy! Let's be passionate! Let's try to stay awake past eleven!"

Seeing how you two looked at each other really tells the story.

Remembering a Valentine,
Sandee

2/16/94
Dear Mama,

On this day many years ago, you struggled so hard to bring me into the world. Today, I focused on a picture of my childhood. You remember, the one with you, me and Mammaw Fiew. When I look at this picture, a long time feeling of peace fills my heart.

But my favorite picture of you was taken on our trip to Europe. Just looking at it brings a smile to my face. We did have a wonderful time, didn't we?

Because today is my birthday, I longed to read what you wrote on a card of days gone by. You said in one of them, "Your mother loves you and I believe you are a treasure . . . a blessing from above. You grow dearer each year."

In the card you gave me last year, you wrote, "It is so wonderful to have a lovely caring daughter and to also have a best friend. You are greatly loved." Truly you were my very best friend. I was very blessed in having you as a mother. To have had such a difficult beginning on my day of birth, we had a lovely ending.

Your Loving Daughter,
Sandee

3/5/94
Dear Mama,

I really need to have courage today. I need my mama's type of courage to continue to sort through your things and to face the grief ahead. All day long I have looked at two pictures that remind me of your courage. One is of Tim and Joy's wedding when you left the hospital bed with pneumonia to attend the service. If I look real hard, I can see the IV needle behind the wrist bouquet.

The other picture was taken on a day of even greater courage. You left the hospital only days after the tumor was removed from your spine and went directly to the reception honoring you and Dad with the naming of Williams Hall at Luther Rice Seminary. You donned that neck brace with such dignity. It was a day of rejoicing.

God grant me the courage needed to meet all the tomorrow.

In His Name,
Sandee

5/8/94

Dear Mama,

This year there are many firsts for all of us. So, today is not only my first Mother's Day without you, but also the first time your birthday has passed since you are gone. Every time I heard a commercial on TV or the radio advertising Mother's Day, I would take a deep breath so as not to cry.

I was in a checkout line the other day when the lady in front of me coarsely said to the teller, "Last year, I forgot Mother's Day. I didn't get my mother a present. Guess I'd better get something this year." I closed my eyes and thought, I'll never be able to give my mama a Mother's Day gift again, or a birthday present.

It's so hard to be without you.

But I have such wonderful memories. The pictures of Randy, Tim and me as children cause my mind to flood with such pleasant thoughts. And then, look at the pictures of us all grown up. You liked that picture of me because it reminded you of your mother. The picture of Randy is the one taken to be placed on the Pastors' Wall at First Baptist Church, Tampa. And the one of Tim was taken on Bourbon Street, as Tim was leading a young man to the Lord during the Southern Baptist Convention. Amazingly, it appeared on the front page of the Dallas Morning News.

None of us could have been what we are without you—our "wind beneath our wings."

Thank You For Your Sacrifice,
Sandee

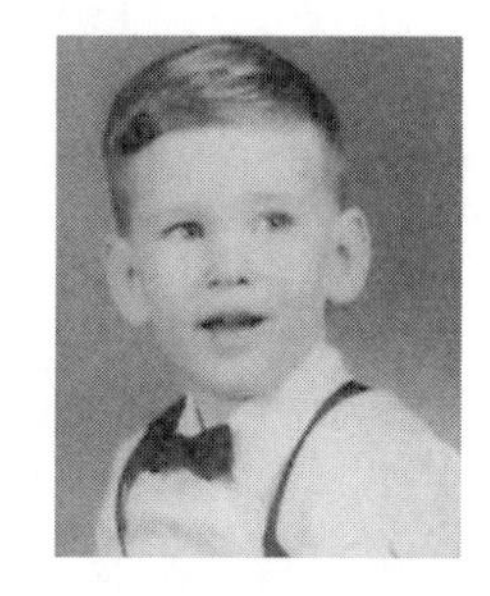

5/20/94
Dear Mama,

I had dinner with Dad the other day at your favorite restaurant, the Victoria House. I think he's doing better, even though he misses you greatly. Dad said to me, "If someone doesn't hurt over the loss of one they loved, then I wonder if they really, really loved them. Surely, if there was a great love between them, the loss would be great and the suffering would be penetrating."

By the way, I ran across the last picture taken of you and Dad. It was this summer in the mountains. Dad, as always, thought you were gorgeous. And he was right.

I Love You My Dear Mama,
Sandee

8/1/94
Dear Mama,

Do you remember Bettye at the Conyers Pet Store? Well, a few days ago her dog had three puppies. The only problem was that the mother dog rejected the newborn babies. She refused to care for them or nurse them.

But something very interesting happened. Bettye's cat had kittens on the very same day and that cat took into her litter the three orphaned puppies. It's a most unique sight to see kittens and puppies being cleaned, nursed and carried around by a cat.

Of all the things God must look after in this vast world, it is beautiful to think He took time to care for three little puppies. Mama, you taught me as a child that God has His eye on the sparrow and if He cared for a sparrow, then He surely cared for me.

This thought indeed has kept me going during these most difficult months because I was constantly reminded that God cared even for me. Through those gut-wrenching days, my belief system said there was hope but my heart felt hopeless. So, I began to pray, "Heal my heart. Lord, heal my heart."

Mama, I watched you die. Although death is a part of life, the memories of you dying are penetrating. I knew you didn't want to die.

Even to the end, you fought hard to stay alive. Yet, it was clear you were not afraid to die. You faced death as you had faced life—with anticipation.

In life, you always said you had "one foot on the road." You were always ready to go at the drop of a hat. In fact, I think your parents misnamed you. Instead of Dorothy Jo, they should have called you Dorothy "Go" because you were always ready to go on to the next adventure in life, no matter if it were good or bad. This was even seen in you attitude of "living" with cancer.

It was kind of like your entire life was a hitch-hike to heaven and you hopped on the Jesus Express. It was because Christ lived in your heart, that you died with hope and expectation.

And it's the Christ in me that causes me to live today with the same hope and expectation. In Christ, we shall be together again. Indeed, life in Christ is real. And yes, there is hope.

My heart is now healing. And I know that even though the pink marble finally came in—Mama, it still ain't over! We'll be together again in the Sweet Bye and Bye.

With Love,
Sandee

How to order more copies of

"Mama, it ain't over 'til the pink marble comes"

and obtain a free Hannibal Books catalog

FAX: 1-972-487-7960

Call: 1-800-747-0738 (in Texas, 1-972-487-5710)

Email: hannibalbooks@earthlink.net

Mail copy of form below to:

Hannibal Books
P.O. Box 461592
Garland, Texas 75046

Visit: www.hannibalbooks.com

Number of copies desired ________________
Multiply number of copies by $9.95 ___X___$9.95___
Cost of books: $__________

Please add $3 for postage and handling for first book and add 50-cents for each additional book in the order.

Shipping $__________
Texas residents add 8.25 % sales tax $__________

Total order $__________

Mark method of payment:
check enclosed ______________________________
Credit card# ____________________ exp. date__________
(Visa, MasterCard, Discover, American Express accepted)

Name ______________________________

Address ______________________________

City State, Zip ______________________________

Phone ____________________ FAX ____________________

Email ______________________________

These inspiring books are also available

Rescue by Jean Phillips. American missionaries Jean Phillips and husband Gene lived through some of the most harrowing moments in African history of the last half century. Abducted and threatened with death, Jean and Gene draw on God's lessons of a lifetime.

______**Copies at $12.95=**_______

Unmoveable Witness by Marion Corley. An alarming interrogation by Colombia's version of the FBI. A dangerous mishap at a construction site. A frightening theft at his home in Bucaramanga, Colombia. What kept Marion and Evelyn Corley on the mission field for 22 years when others might have returned to Stateside comforts?

_______**Copies at $9.95=**_______

Awaken the Dawn by Doris B. Wolfe. Christian romance novel set in the jungles of South America involving two missionaries, one a recent widower with two children and the other a young, never-married single woman. He's a pilot. She's a teacher. Dramatic real-life situations test their faith.

_______**Copies at $9.95=**_______

The Jungle series, also known as the Rani Adventures by Ron Snell. With hilarity, warmth, and spine-tingling suspense, "the Rani Series" trilogy takes readers into the cross-cultural upbringing of Ron Snell, who, with his family, sets aside American comforts to bring the good news of Christ to people in darkness in the Amazon jungles of Peru.

It's a Jungle Out There (Book 1) ______ **Copies at $7.95 =** ________
Life is a Jungle (Book 2) ______ **Copies at $7.95 =** ________
Jungle Calls (Book 3) ______ **Copies at $7.95 =** ________

Add $3.00 shipping for first book, plus 50-cents for each additional book.
Shipping & Handling ____________
Texas residents add 8.25% sales tax ________
TOTAL ENCLOSED____________

check ____ or credit card # ___________________ exp. date_____
(Visa, MasterCard, Discover, American Express accepted)

Name ____

Address ____________________________ Phone ____________

City ____________________ State ____________ Zip __________

For postal address, phone number, fax number, email address and other ways to order from Hannibal Books, see page 191